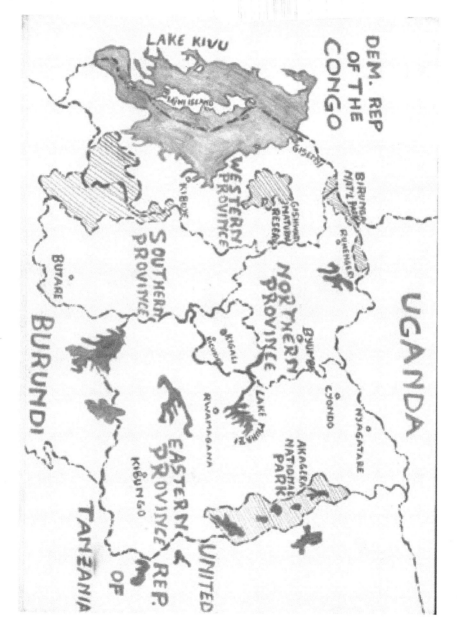

Embracing Survival

A Memoir

By Dydine Umunyana

Edited by Elizabeth Evans

UMBRELLA PRESS, LLC

California USA

No Foreign sky protected me,
no stranger's wing shielded my face.
I stand as witness to the common lot,
survivor of that time, that place.

Anna Akhmatova

Published by Umbrella Press, LLC
Po BOX: 5694 Santa Monica, California USA, 90409
Embracing Survival

Edited by: Elizabeth Evans
Co Edited by: Barbara Kraft
Cover Design: Arno Michaelis
Cover profile photos: Murenzi Kamatari
Rwanda Map Art: Basil Boris Kanyamibwa
Photos by Michele Zousmer on Page 251, 264, 271

Library of Congress Control Number: 2016911303
ISBN: 978-0-9977704-0-7 (Paperback)
ISBN: 978-0-9977704-1-4 (Clothbound)
eISBN: 978-0-9977704-2-1

Cover image: Students at Washington High School of Information Technology in Milwaukee, Wisconsin created a fiber-arts portrait of Dydine Umunyana along with artist-in-residence, Vanessa Andrews. The portrait is made of multiple layers of denim jean fabric, inspired by the student's study of Denim Day, and women of influence around the globe (including Dydine Umunyana!) Who work to level the playing field for women and girls across all aspects of society. **Original Photograph:** Jonathan Kloberdanz

The project was made possible by Arts @ Large's Serve2Unite Student Leadership Chapters. Arts @ Large, Inc. is a nationally-recognized educational organization that builds the skills, confidence, and competence of classroom teachers, arts specialists, and artist educators to engage thousands of students annually in experiential, arts-infused learning

For more Information: www.dydine.com
Printed in United States of America
Dydine Umunyana, First U.S.edition 2016

Table of content

Praise

Dear Dydine,

Thank you for sharing your manuscript. I've been working on a writing project, too, and began reading your story with the intent of reading it in bits and pieces during breaks from my writing. That turned out to be impossible. Your story was too gripping to put down and I finished it in couple of days.

Your storytelling is amazing. Telling your story through a child's eyes made it all the more poignant. As horrifying as much of your story is to read, I was compelled to keep reading and hoping for things to get better and for you and your siblings to be safe. It was an awfully long wait. Having read other works about the genocide and having seen several films, I found your story unique in several ways.

The child's eye view is very powerful and personal. I can envision in my mind's eye your story portrayed on film, following this child through her struggles. Your portrayal of PTSD was accurate and insightful. This is perhaps the most horrible legacy of the genocide, passing the pain from generation to generation. It is epidemic in your country and the main reason I visited Rwanda in the first place.

You portrayed all the consequences of trauma that accompany PTSD, including particularly substance dependence and domestic violence. During my visit in 2013, I got to know our driver, whose story was much like your father's. He was fundamentally a good man, but was addicted to alcohol and abusive to his family when drunk or having flashbacks. One of my colleagues has tried very hard to help him, but to the best of my knowledge he and his family still suffer.

My wife and I have supported Partners in Health, which works in Rwanda to provide medical and psychiatric care. With our financial help, they have begun to include trauma, substance dependence, and domestic violence in the programs they are developing. In the US and much of Europe, one of the most powerful interventions for substance dependence is Alcoholics Anonymous. This is a self-help group with meetings scheduled daily or more in communities all over the world. The Twelve Steps of Alcoholics Anonymous is a system of recovery based on a combination of faith, mindfulness, and mutual help.

Your book might be of value in breaking through people's reluctance to share their stories and perhaps enable AA to gain a foothold in Rwanda, where it is crucial to reach large numbers of people with low cost interventions. (Unlike formal treatment, AA is free.

I think your book will be widely read. It is beautifully written and emotionally evocative. Endings are often difficult to write and I particularly liked the final two paragraphs of your Afterword, a very satisfying conclusion.

Rick Moskovitz

Dydine,

I wanted to send a note to tell you I finished reading your book. Despite the weight and severity of your subject, it was a genuine pleasure getting to know you all over again across the span of these well drafted pages. It seems one great gift of literature is it's ability to transmit subjectivity in a way that no amount of conversation, or even shared experience, can. You have put down a personal, emotional and historical record that can stand the test of time, that can and will speak for you in ways you will no longer have to. I have walked some miles in your shoes, and they have left me humbled, moved and inspired. One of life's more benevolent ironies, it seems to me, is that the more we expose the things that hurt us, the more powerful we become, the more ways we offer people to love us. Sunlight is a powerful disinfectant. I imagine the response has already been quite powerful, and I hope you enjoy it. It is infinitely deserved.

With much love and admiration,

Sean

Author's Note

"Please don't go, at least stay with me for a little longer and help me cry, because my own tears will never be enough for my family". I heard this quote when I was a little girl. My dad was asking my mom to stay. It never left my heart.

This is a work of a nonfiction about my life, spanning over twenty years since the time I was born. As you might expect, certain conversations have been recreated as they were described to me, or have been paraphrased from memory to the best of my ability. In some instances, names of individuals have been changed in order to preserve their anonymity. Or the timeline has been compressed to make for a more engaging read. Although I wish they were not, all the stories conveyed here are true.

Prologue

My country was once called the land of milk and honey, but overnight it has become a land of blood and sorrow. I'm lined up with many other Tutsi people in the front yard of one of the Hutu perpetrators. We have all been captured. We are waiting to learn our fate. Only minutes ago I was separated from my family, amidst hundreds of Tutsis fleeing for their safety. I'm still clutching the jar of milk I was drinking when my Auntie Agnes rushed my cousins and me out of the house into the street. We were racing to the church for safety, but so was everyone else. I look down and see dead bodies at my feet. In the distance, people wail as they are being slaughtered. Whistles, blown by Hutus celebrating the massacre, echo across the hills.

My small body trembles. I am sweating. I am just a child. What have I done to be hunted this way? It feels like something big is about to happen. A growing sense of anxiety swells inside my stomach.

My captors tower over me like a group of angry giants. They are drenched in blood and look like malumba (demons) in horror movies. I am not very scared because this house is familiar. It belongs to one of my neighbors, and I am friends with their children. I am too young to know what death means, to understand the difference between good and evil. Yet, as I look around, dead bodies are everywhere.

I'm not quite four years old, and the only little person in line with many other adult Tutsis. The Hutu Interahamwe ("those who attack together") begin moving down the line, slaughtering people with machetes one by one. I shake harder. The sounds people make as they die are horrifying. Now, I know for sure that something is wrong. Tears flow down my cheeks. The Interahamwe are getting so close to me. I am next for sure. All I can do is close my eyes. I feel this might be the last moment of my life.

The Interahamwe pause. One of them gestures toward me.

"This is a child of RPF Inkotanyi Soldiers! A child of snakes is a snake itself. She is a cockroach, kill her! Her mother and father are in RPF Inkotanyi. Kill her, kill her!"

Being a person whose parents are in RPF Inkotanyi, or the Rwanda Patriotic Front, seems to be the worst thing I could be. I feel guilty, like I have made a mistake, or there is something wrong with me.

They start to argue with one another.

"I am the one who is going to kill her," one guard says to another.

"No! I will be the one to make her suffer. Her parents and uncles are our worst enemies!"

They are yelling so loud, and they all want the honor of finishing me off. One of the men arguing grows frustrated and impatient. Without any agreement between himself and the other Interahamwe, he rushes towards me with a machete and a crude homemade weapon called Ntamponganoyumwanzi, which literally translates to "no pity for the enemy."

With a timid voice I ask, "Would you please let me drink my milk?" Growing up, according to what I learned from my Auntie Agnes, if a child wants to have something to eat or drink, an adult has to be asked first. One of the men starts mimicking me, snickering loudly with the other Interahamwe. With a smirk on his face he mocks me, "Would you please let me drink my milk?" The other men join in with him, "Oh, of course you can have your milk, darling, you would not be a Tutsi child, a real cockroach, if you didn't ask for milk! Hahahahah!"

Terrified, I raise the jar to my lips, but I am so scared that I cannot drink. As I do this, the Interahamwe discuss in which way they are going to make me suffer before they kill me. I am terrified by these horrible giants, covered in blood. I will never forget the stench of the smell.

As I fake drinking, an elderly Hutu man steps out from inside the house. He sees me standing in the line where those before me have died. Those who are still alive are badly beaten by machetes, and barely breathing. I am confused and terrified. Nothing makes sense.

The elderly man scolds the executioners, "Why aren't you doing your work? You are wasting time!" In response, his eldest son, the leader of this Interahamwe group, speaks, "This is Mapuwa's daughter." Suddenly the older man's eyes grow with familiarity and with a sudden change of heart, he speaks again. "You should be ashamed of killing an innocent child like this one, while your wives have children no different from her. No one touch her, or you will have to go through me first!"

Both men rush toward me, one to save me, the other to put me to death. This was the very first morning of Tutsi genocide, Rwanda, April 7th, 1994, and the worst was yet to come.

Chapter One: Welcome to the World

My name is Dydine Umunyana. This is my story, but it does not belong solely to me. It is the story of my parents' choices, of our family's survival, and of all Rwandans whose lives were brutally interrupted and forever changed when a hundred day madness seized our country in 1994. What has become known as the Rwandan Genocide Against the Tutsis occurred From the afternoon of April 6th to mid-July 1994. Hutu extremists attacked and murdered neighboring Tutsis and moderate Hutus, seeking their extermination. An estimated one million Rwandans were killed, roughly 20% of the overall population and 70% of the Tutsi population.

I was a child then, not even able to tie my own shoes, and to me the violence was confusing and terrifying. Little did I know then that resentment between the Tutsis and Hutus had been brewing for generations, and this was not the first time it had exploded into violence to claim the lives of those in my family. I was 18 years old when I learned that my own great grandfather had been crucified in the wake of the 1959 Rwandan Revolution at Muhazi Lake. His crime: being Tutsi.

Many point to the 1959 Revolution as the beginning of the civil war between the Tutsis and Hutus, but to truly understand the conflict we must reach back much further in time. Rwanda is an ancient land, and it is believed that the first inhabitants, the Twa people, settled here in 700B.C. Over the centuries, other groups migrated to the region. The people coalesced, intermarried, and shared one language and culture. Rwanda, a small country with an overwhelmingly agricultural economy, had one of the highest population densities in Africa.

There were no separate tribes or ethnic groups, but the terms Twa, Hutu and Tutsi emerged to differentiate between social classes. "Tutsi" referred to the more prosperous class of cattle herders, whereas "Hutu" referred to those who farmed the land. Eventually, Tutsi came to refer broadly to the elite, ruling class.

If animosity or mistrust existed between the social classes in the Rwandan kingdom's early years, it was stirred and stoked by the arrival of European colonialists in the late eighteenth century. Rwanda was first colonized by the Germans, then by the Belgians after the First World War. The Europeans' idea of material and economic status became of significant importance, and they began to designate Rwanda's social classes into ethnic groups in order to divide and control them. In reality though, there were no tribes.

Prior to these artificial designations, a Hutu, by acquiring wealth, could become a Tutsi. But now that changed. The Europeans determined which class a person belonged to by measuring height, facial features and generally arbitrary characteristics. In 1935, Rwandan citizens were given identification cards labeling them as Tutsi, Hutu, Twa or Naturalized.

Believing the wealthier Tutsis were originally migrants from Ethiopia, and were thus more Caucasian and racially superior to the Hutus, the Belgians favored the minority Tutsis over the Hutus and created a legacy of tension. They concentrated the country's lands with the Tutsis, often stripping Hutus of their property with little or no compensation. As Tutsi power and wealth expanded, the Hutus became disenfranchised, and were often forced by the government to work as labor as the country rapidly modernized. At this time, Belgium governed Rwanda through the ruling Tutsi King Musinga, but as the tide of Hutu unrest grew, Belgium saw the writing on the wall. Fearing rebellion, they switched allegiance to the Hutu and withdrew their support of the Tutsis.

A Hutu revolution in 1959 forced as many as 300,000 Tutsis to flee the country. On a visit to neighboring Burundi, King Musinga was poisoned and killed. When his son, Prince Kigeri, seized his father's position, he was hunted alongside the rest of the Tutsi population. King Kigeri and thousands of other Tutsis fled to neighboring countries for their safety in exile. For the next three decades, the Tutsis who survived and stayed in Rwanda lived in fear. The Hutus took over power in the government, and taught their children to hate the Tutsis. By early 1961, victorious Hutus declared the country a republic. After a U.N. referendum that same year, Belgium officially granted independence to Rwanda in July 1962.

Ethnically motivated violence continued in the decades following independence, as Tutsi refugees living abroad agitated to return to Rwanda, launching attacks against the Hutu Government that were met with swift retaliation. It was midst this growing chaos that I arrived in this world. But to properly understand my story, we must first begin with the story of my mother, Devota.

Devota lived in the heart of Africa, in Rwamagana, a small village surrounded by emerald hills, close to a gorgeous natural lake called Muhazi. My mother was considered a great beauty. She was tall and carried herself with confidence. She was a pre school teacher. Our neighbors affectionately called her by her childhood nickname Mapuwa and knew her by her ever-present smile.

In her youth Devota reveled in the beauty of the natural world. She loved to catch butterflies, smell flowers, and tip her head back to marvel at the glory of the sky. Sometimes the magic of it all overwhelmed her. At sunset, she would cry with appreciation for the grace of God. No matter what life brought her, whether it was sadness, joy, or a broken heart, she vowed never to let her smile fade.

It is hard for me to imagine my mother so young and carefree. The innocence of her youth did not last long. The year was nineteen ninety and my mother Devota was nineteen years old, pregnant with me and without a husband. One night, as she gazed down at her growing belly, she realized she could not hide her secret from her family anymore.

She lived with her two parents, Madeline and Yohana, and was the eighth child born of twelve. The family was Tutsi, and relatively well off within the community. They owned a plantain plantation in the hills behind their home. Out of Devota's four sisters, only the eldest, Josephine, had been married. Devota was in love with her boyfriend, Laurent, a kind, intelligent young man whose family was from Ruhengeri in the Northern Province. He was called away by his work.

A mathematician and language translator working for Rwandan law enforcement (Gendarme), he was assigned to Kibungo, in the Eastern Province and that's how he met my mother. Laurent and his family were also Tutsi. Devota's parents approved of Laurent but refused to let them marry. Culturally, a woman was not permitted to marry before her elder sisters wed. Devota decided that no matter what, she would marry Laurent. To encourage her parent's blessing, she took matters into her own hands, and became pregnant. Her actions did not have the desired effect.

When her family learned of the pregnancy, they shunned her and refused to speak to her. As in many parts of the world, an unplanned pregnancy was a nightmare for a teenager in Rwanda. According to the culture, a child born out of wedlock is a failure to the family. It spiritually disrupts the course of the entire family, as well as the community. My mother knew all this before she became pregnant, but she simply didn't believe her family would turn against her. When they did, it shook her to her core.

Overnight, my mother had gone from being the family's pride to its source of shame. The smile faded from her lips. Feeling she was a disappointment to her parents was unbearable. She could only find peace when she walked away from the village far into the hills. Sometimes she would wander alone for hours at a time. The girlfriends she grew up with avoided her. If she came upon them laughing and singing, they would go silent and turn their backs to her.

My father Laurent in his early twenties stood by Devota, but had nothing yet to provide for a family. She was still dependent upon her parents, even if they refused to speak her name. The situation was agony, but Devota committed herself to a decision. She would keep her baby, and no one would be able to change her mind.

Months passed, and then one night, around midnight, Devota woke up, feeling the urge to use the bathroom. She was distracted on her way outside and stood in the doorway of her home looking into the starry darkness and fields of fireflies. An illuminated crescent moon shined upon her. She was sweating, though the night air was cold. Her knees shook, and she realized she couldn't walk herself all the way to the toilet. Instead, she turned toward the plantain farm behind her older sister Josephine's house. As she moved, she felt something unusual, like something was hitting her from inside her womb.

She fell to the ground, sitting, and talking to herself. She knew what she had to do. *There is no turning back now,* she thought, *you must go through with this.* Devota had no idea how to give birth. She knew nothing about it, and no one had prepared her. Her eyes bulged wildly as she gasped for air. She let out a penetrating scream that woke the neighborhood.

Everyone woke in a panic and ran to see what was happening. At first they thought someone was being attacked. Rumors of war were all over the country's radio. Tutsis were being threatened and beaten, often jailed, on suspicion of supporting the Rwanda Patriotic Front, or RPF Inkotanyi. Founded by Tutsis living in exile in Uganda since the 1959 Revolution, the RPF Inkotanyi was fighting to return to their rightful home in Rwanda. Lately, skirmishes between the RPF Inkotanyi and Hutu government had been coming alarmingly close to the village.

By the time the villagers reached Devota, the baby was already falling onto the bananas leaves. When Devota's sister, Josephine, came outside the baby was already crying. Taking the baby from the cold, Devota held the baby close to her heart, and smiled a happy, yet nervous smile. "I did it," she said. "It's a baby girl!" This is the story of how I came into this world.

Wondering what would happen to us next, my mother searched the faces of those surrounding her. She could sense they all wanted to be close to her and the new member of their community, but they knew Devota was unwelcome. She would have to find a new place to live. The faces of her mother,

Madeline and neighbors became disturbed. Eventually, they left her there, slowly wandering back to their homes. Only Devota's sister Josephine felt compassion in her heart for her little sister. She took her inside her house, as my mother thanked her. "It's only temporary," Josephine replied.

Baby Dydine

Chapter Two: The Exile

Our "temporary" stay with my Auntie Josephine's family gradually became more permanent. Shortly after my birth, my father had hatched a plan for him, my mother and me to live together. He continued to support me and my mother, but we seldom saw him. I have no memories of him from those early months.

My Auntie could not bear to turn my mother out. And so for the first two years of my life, I grew up happily amidst a tumble of cousins, watched over by the extended family, unaware I was different from anyone else. Eventually, not even my grandparents could keep their distance and I became a favorite of my grandfather, who always brought me bananas when he went to the village center. Our home life was a happy one, but trouble lurked outside our door.

In 1992, two years after I was born, a chaotic chain of events took place in Rwanda. Forces of the RPF Inkotanyi, consisting mostly of Tutsi refugees, invaded Rwanda from Uganda in October 1990. The Hutu government threatened the RPF Inkotanyi that if they continued fighting for their re-entry in the country, the military would retaliate against the Tutsis living within Rwanda. This is exactly what happened. The government killed thousands of Tutsis living inside the country, including my Uncle Karasira, my father's younger brother, who was 31 years old. He was arrested by one of many Hutu militias and, like many other Tutsis, was accused of being a spy along with his 28 year old younger brother, my Uncle Safari, who at the time was home for the Christmas holiday from medical School.

Vermin. Cockroaches. This is what the Hutu perpetrators called us. They dehumanized the Tutsis so they felt justified treating their captives as trash. Conditions in the prison were notoriously bad, and my father's mother feared the worst. With her two young sons in custody, my grandmother made an arrangement with one of the prison guards she knew from her village. She offered him a hefty bribe for both sons, but the Guard arranged only for my Uncle Safari's escape but not for my Uncle Karasira.

He told the two brothers that Karasira was too well known in the community and when the execution time would come Karasira's absence would be noticed and the guard would be killed. Uncle Safari, who had been away at school, was not known as well. The guard arranged for Safari to leave but Karasira had to remain and was indeed shortly executed there after.

Across the country in the Eastern Province of Rwanda Province, my father Laurent sat in a bar across from a group of Hutu officers. He worked with the officers and tried to remain on good terms with them, but the friendship was uneasy. The situation for Tutsis seemed to be worsening by the day, and befriending Hutus seemed a necessary form of security, even if it was a distasteful one. Laurent cracked a joke, and a couple of the Hutu men laughed, but they seemed distracted.

One of the men exchanged a knowing glance with the others. "Hey, Laurent, you hear about your brother?" he asked, tipping back in his chair. An icy shiver traveled down Laurent's spine. He forced a smile, and shook his head, feigning nonchalance.

"What was his name?" the man turned to the officer beside him. "Ah, yes, Karasira." He looked Laurent in the eye. "He's dead. Tortured and executed in prison. You'll never see him again." The man chuckled and drained his beer.

Laurent's entire body went numb. Karasira? It was incomprehensible he wouldn't see his brother again. How long had the men known? His supposed friends had taken him to the bar and sat down with him to drink, and all along they had known. It had been a set up, he realized, for their amusement. Rage swelled inside him. There was no more faking niceties. There was no friendship. He sprung from his chair and lunged at the man across from him, but the others were on him in an instant. They wrestled him to the ground, shoving his head against the floor. His cheek pressed to the cool concrete, Laurent wept for his brother. More Hutu officers arrived to take him away. They beat him and threw him in jail, where he remained for over a year. He was never able to grieve his brother's death with the rest of his family.

When my mother learned the news of Laurent's imprisonment, she was consumed with worry but there was little she could do. When he was released, my mother rushed to his side. They wanted be together, to put everything behind them and start a proper family, but the reality was this was not a good time to settle down. Weeks after my father was released, he was attacked by another group of Hutu extremists, who tried to beat him to death. He survived, and fled to join the RPF Inkotanyi, which was his only choice as a young Tutsi man. That time. Within weeks of his departure, my mother Devota found out that she was pregnant again.

My Auntie Josephine was extremely disappointed when she learned my mother was pregnant again without a husband. She had been hosting us for years. Josephine was reserved and soft spoken by nature, and she didn't express her opinions freely. Naturally averse to conflict, she was no match for my mother in an argument. But even Josephine had her limits. We were having dinner together at the dining room table one evening: me, my mother, Auntie Josephine, and her four children. A small oil lamp on the table flickered in the darkness.

"Devota, how are you going to do this?" Josephine asked. "You know for sure that the government is going to come here any day now in search of Laurent."

The fact was that my and my mother's presence in her home was endangering Josephine's entire family. Now that my father had joined RPF Inkotanyi, we were all considered suspicious. My mother stood up at the table, furious with her sister. She wanted to let her have it. How could Josephine add to her troubles? As if she didn't have enough to worry about right now. Suddenly, an abrupt knock rang out. A man's voice boomed from behind the front door,

"Open up right now! Where is your husband? He needs to show his face now, or things are going to get worse for everyone here!"

Josephine immediately opened the door and a group of Hutu men rushed inside the house. When they couldn't find my father, they took away my mother instead. They would interrogate her until she could explain Laurent's whereabouts.

After that evening, and all throughout her pregnancy, my mother was constantly taken into interrogation. She started to lose hope for her life, and the future of her country. It had been ages since she'd had word of Laurent. What kind of world would her children be brought up in? Would her family ever be united?

There are letters that contain words that should never be read. Letters that are in themselves terrible acts of cruelty. We were not with my father when he received the letter from the Hutu gendarme. It pains me to think that he was alone when he learned the unspeakable details of his brother's death. It was an official letter explaining how Karasira was killed. How he was tortured and executed without dignity.

The Hutu militias took everyone in the same jail into the Volcano Mountains, the rugged chain of five volcanoes in Ruhengeri. They chopped off every part of their bodies, one by one. They cut Karasira's arms from his shoulders so he could fit in a long pit where nobody would ever find his body. He was still alive when they threw him in, when they tossed the other bodies, which no longer looked like human bodies, on top of him. This is how he died. His body was never found.

The letter described, in painstaking detail, the whole process of how that inhuman, horrible event transpired. It was written matter of factly, without apology, and I wonder if this letter is what began the change in my father. Perhaps the pain of it was so unthinkable that for my father human decency ceased to exist.

A few months after the birth of my baby brother, Fils, things got worse for the Tutsis in Rwanda. One of my mother's old friends, now a Catholic Priest living within Rwamagana Cathedral, told her to find a safe place where she could leave her children and flee the country, or she would be the cause of her family's death. The Priest had heard that she might be killed because of government speculations that she was sending information to the RPF Inkotanyi through Laurent.

More terrified now than ever before, my mother took us with her on a night bus to the Northern province in Ruhengeri, where my father's family lived, to beg his relatives to take us in.

"Oh, this is my Umunyana," my grandmother said, grinning as we met for the first time. Gently, she touched my cheek. "She is Umunyana." My grandmother gave me my name, which means something you see once in a lifetime that brings you good luck.

She fawned over me, her kindly face inches from mine. "Look at her smile. She looks just like my son, her Uncle

Safari." She turned to my brother and took him from my mother's arms, holding him close to her chest. With so much love, she said, "You, you are Kanamugire," my father's last name. She called my father's whole family to come and meet us. She had eight children remaining, most of whom were married and lived with their families close by. My uncles and aunties were so happy to meet me and my brother, especially my Auntie Uwamahoro, who was sixteen years old, and my father's youngest sibling. It was an exciting day until Devota told my grandmother the reason for our visit.

"No, Devota," my grandmother said gently, shaking her head. "You can't leave your kids here, my dear daughter-in-law. I love you but you have to listen to me very carefully. I have a bad feeling that something big is about to happen, and these two little angels might be the only blood of my family who are going to survive. Please take them away from here."

My mother was so upset that my grandmother did not want us, that without saying a word, we were back on the bus to Rwamagana. My mother knew that she had to leave the country as soon as possible, but that my brother and I had to stay. She feared that none of us were going to survive if she stayed any longer. We were on our way to my Grandma Madeline's house. My mother dropped us off, and I remember her telling me that she was going to the market to buy me some bananas, and that she would be back soon. She never returned that day.

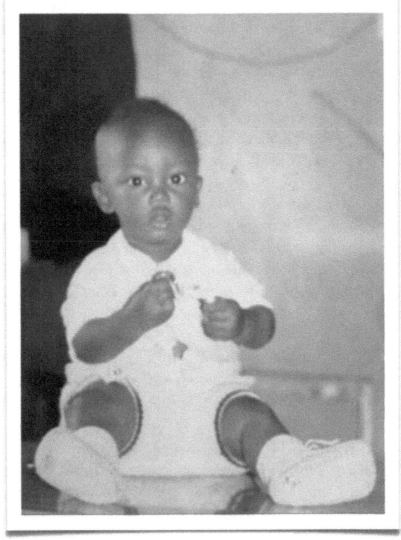

Baby Fils

Chapter Three: We Miss Them Terribly

I waited for my mother to come back for my brother and me. I clung to the memory of her voice, telling me, "I'm going to the market to buy you some bananas, Sweetheart Dydine, and I will be back in a minute." After she disappeared, I would occasionally overhear snippets of conversation from people who came to visit my grandma. "My God!" They'd say. "We've heard that Mapuwa has joined RPF Inkotanyi! Do you know what the Inkotanyi look like? They are green, and they have horns, long ears and tails. This is what Devota will look like the next time we see her. She is not your daughter anymore. She is now a cockroach... she is a snake, just like all other RPF Inkotanyi."

I do not know whether these people meant to be cruel. I believe they were simply careless. They parroted what they heard on the media. There was so much war propaganda against the RPF Inkotanyi and Tutsis at that time, on the news, on the radio, in politician's speeches, that all people, Tutsi as well as Hutu, were tempted to believe even the most sensational rumors. They weren't telling my grandmother anything new. They wanted to gossip, they weren't thinking of my grandmother's pain.

Grandma was always polite. She welcomed everyone in and offered them food. By this time, three of my grandparents' children had left to join the RPF, including two of my mother's older brothers. Grandma could be a tough imperious woman, the queen of the house, but she still cared a lot about what other people thought. Family pride was important to her, and I imagine it was humiliating for her to have three of her children referred to as cockroaches.

When the sun set, my brother, my cousins and I knew it was story time. This was the most exciting time of day for us. We would sit together on a straw mat watching the sun go down and the stars come up, surrounding my Grandpa's feet as he sat on his throne-like traditional wooden stool. My Grandpa Yohana Baptiste was hard working with a gentle, easy-going demeanor. He always spoke softly, in a voice that was calming and low. He worked in the fields everyday, even in his later years when he carried a cane. A man of simple pleasures, he liked to come home in the evenings and smoke tobacco and sit with his grandchildren.

When we went to bed, he'd head to the local bar to share beer and stories with his friends. I begged him for stories about my mother. He would try not to make eye contact with me, to avoid having to answer all my questions, but I was relentless.

"Grandpa, where did my mother like to play with us? Why did she leave us? Did she not like us?"

Grandpa had a lot of hard questions to answer. He told me how Devota loved me, how my brother and I were her favorites, about the places we used to play together, and how one day she would come back for us.

"Your mother loved to teach you how to walk across the fallen Eucalyptus in the street. It is over a hundred years old. It fell down on the sidewalk ten years ago, because it was so old. Your mother spent so much time on that tree laughing about how you couldn't walk and how you were wobbling from side to side. I loved seeing her with her beautiful smile." Grandpa said this with tears in his eyes.

There is a proverb in Rwandan culture that says that men's tears flow into their stomachs, not down their faces. It is meant to indicate their strength, that men do not reveal their weakness. Like a true Rwandan man, Grandpa held his tears in check. The more I heard about my mother, the more questions I had about my father. The only answer I could get from anyone was that my dad was a very smart, loving person and he loved both my baby brother Fils and me. I heard this all the time, and it only made me more curious and hopeful that one day I would meet him. I imagined how beautiful it would be for my family to be together.

Time passed, and I grew into an inquisitive and independent three year old. I developed a strong affection for the eucalyptus tree in the road outside the house, and some of my first memories are of sitting alone on that tree, sometimes with Simba, my grandmother's dog, waiting for my mother's return. I thought one day she might come back for me, and I would be the first one to welcome her. My Auntie Agnes, the third of my grandparents' daughters, hated seeing me on that tree, because she would always find me crying silently to myself. Agnes was a devoted Christian. She never liked to see me, or anyone else, sad, even as the violence against Tutsi families escalated daily.

In August 1993, the Hutu President Juvenal Habyarimana signed a ceasefire agreement at Arusha, Tanzania, calling for the creation of a transition government that would include the RPF Inkotanyi. This power-sharing agreement angered Hutu extremists, who took swift and horrible action against the Tutsis inside Rwanda. My Auntie Agnes feared it was becoming unsafe for a child my age to be outdoors alone. In spite of her gentle coaxing, I refused to abandon my post.

Thursdays were an especially exciting time to watch from the tree. Every Thursday people passed by on their way to the farmer's market at the village center, where people from all over Eastern Province gathered with their goods. Sometimes I would see someone or hear a voice and think it was my mom, but in reality, it was just my imagination, and would always turn out to be someone else.

I missed my mother everyday, especially when I saw other kids with their parents. The sight of happy families was heartbreaking to me. My grandparents tried everything they could to make me feel better. They loved my brother and me as though we were their own children, and even insisted I call them Dad and Mom. My brother and I were not their only charges. Many of my other cousins, whose parents had also fled the country, lived with my grandparents. I believe there were eight or nine of us all together.

Fils and I were the youngest amongst all the kids, and needed special care, which was hard because our grandparents were old. The childrearing duties largely fell on my Auntie Agnes, who was still single. She had to take care of all of us kids at the same time, even though she knew nothing about parenting. Although she never said so, it was clear that she didn't want the responsibility. She was a woman who wanted everything to be clean and in order. With so many children under one roof, it was an impossible situation.

My grandparents were a rich Tutsi family, so they could afford to care for us all. There were a lot of cows for milk, a large farm area to grow bananas and plantains, and other different vegetables and fruits. My grandparents owned an entire hillside. My grandmother was always home or looking after her staff who worked long hours on the plantation. My grandfather was always with his cows, almost ten miles away from our home. My grandfather loved me very much and had his own nickname only he would call me: Madina.

He always joked that he couldn't pronounce my real name, even though it was not uncommon, and he would say, "Dydine, instead I will call you Madina," with a sly smile. He had already said my name correctly but still refused to admit that he knew how to say Dydine. He was a very funny and peaceful man. After spending his evenings drinking banana beer with his friends, he would come home late, with bananas only for me. Even though he was drunk, he never forgot those bananas.

The bar where my grandfather loved to spend his evenings was in the village center, also called Ikoni. Ikoni is on the main road through Rwanda that goes all the way to Uganda. In the village center, right after the first curve in the road past our house, there was another old Eucalyptus tree where Hutus would gather and hold meetings beneath its branches. This tree was called "Kucyamuvoma" which means "the tree of movement." One night Grandpa became too drunk. He couldn't even walk, and he was drawing figure eights in the street with his feet. His friends told him to go straight home but he didn't listen to them. First, he wanted to buy me those bananas.

It was no longer safe for a Tutsi man to be walking the street late at night. As his friends walked together out of the bar they looked up at the Kucyamuvoma tree and said, "Yohana, these people have been working on the list of Tutsi families who have children in the RPF Inkotanyi, and you might be the first on the list." Where the meeting was happening, my grandfather spat in the dirt. "Those sons of bitches are wasting their time. I'm an old man anyway. Let me go get some bananas for my Madina." He stumbled off into the darkness.

GrandPa Yohana in the white shirt with Joy mom's best friend and Jeacque one of mom's older brothers

Chapter Four: The Crash

On April 6th, 1994, a plane carrying President Habyarimana and Burundi's president Cyprien Ntaryamira was shot down over the interior city of Kigali, leaving no survivors. Our country plunged into chaos. Within an hour of the plane crash, the Presidential Guard, together with members of the Rwandan Armed Forces (FAR) and Hutu militia groups known as the Interahamwe and Impuzamugambi, set up roadblocks and barricades and began slaughtering Tutsis and moderate Hutus with impunity.

Among the first victims were the moderate Hutu Prime Minister Agathe Uwilingiyimana and her ten Belgian bodyguards, killed on April 7th,. The mass killings quickly spread from Kigali to the rest of the country. Local officials and government-sponsored radio stations called on ordinary Rwandan civilians to murder their neighbors.

That same morning of Thursday, April 7th, 1994, I walked, still half-asleep and yawning, into the living room of my grandparents' house. My eyes were barely open, and I desperately wanted to go back to bed, but my Auntie Agnes was waking everyone up. My older cousins sat together on the mat in the living room. Something strange was happening. I looked to see if it was morning, but inside our living room the lantern on the table was lit and no light came through the windows. Auntie Agnes told us not to look outside, and to sit quietly on the floor. She seemed to be the only adult person in the house. I saw no sign of my grandparents. Auntie paced back and fourth, wringing her hands. I had never seen her scared like this before.

I was almost four years old and watched as she puts Fils in a sling on her back, Fils was almost two years old and he stayed asleep. Auntie looked so frustrated. A nervous rage seemed to embody her presence. She was a far different woman from the Auntie Agnes I was used to, the one who hummed happily while doing housework. She looked through the window again and again, as though she were waiting for something or someone to arrive. I looked around at my cousins trying to uncover some information about what was happening, but their expressions were blank. No one dared even whisper. We were all tired and confused.

The silence broke when a voice boomed across our little black Sony radio. "Our president's plane has been shot down by RPF Inkotanyi. Our father has died. In the name of God, his children are to seek revenge and kill all the Snakes and Cockroaches immediately."

Auntie tried to protect us and quickly turned the dial on the radio to another channel, but this emergency warning was blasting on every station, and that hateful voice was the only song we could hear. "Let's get ready, we're going to Rwamagana Cathedral," Auntie Agnes said. I started smiling because my favorite activity was going to church with my family on Sundays. I would get to choose my favorite dress to wear to services.

I spoke up, loud and proud, "I want to wear the dress Grandpa got me last Christmas."

Auntie Agnes whirled around and told me to shut up, which made me start to cry. She put her hand over my mouth and whispered, "What dress is it you want? If you have to say something you whisper from now on, you hear me?"

I looked deeply into her eyes. I'd never seen her this serious. I leaned closer and whispered, "The one that is white with the butterflies."

She disappeared for a moment and returned with the dress, which had three butterflies on the left side, one light pink, one mint green, and one baby blue. When I wore it, they sat next to my heart. In this dress, I was the happiest girl in the world.

Auntie Agnes kept listening to the RTLM (Radio Télévision Libre des Mille Collines) Radio station, and peering out the window. After the radio announcement, my cousins started whispering, and piecing together what was going on. Noise broke out amongst us. "Auntie Agnes, are we going to die?"

"Stop talking!" She snapped. "Nothing is going to happen to you, God cannot allow anything to happen to you." Yet, there was fear on her face. She told us to be absolutely still and quiet, and not to make any noise. If one of us was breathing too loudly, or made even a small cough, her eyes would meet ours with a stern piercing look and we would know what she meant. We had been sitting in the living room for what felt like hours, waiting for the sun to rise, so we could leave the house. Finally, first light came, and Auntie Agnes still had Fils on her back. She instructed the older kids to carry us younger ones, and she organized us into a line, preparing us to leave for the church.

My cousin Mignone, Josephine's daughter, was eight years old, and she held my hand. I clutched a small jar of milk in my other hand. Church was also my Auntie Agnes's favorite activity. Usually when we went it was a joyous occasion, but this time was different. Auntie seemed unsure. No one understood what was going through her mind. As we got outside, the younger kids were happy just to have left the house, but the older ones knew better. Auntie Agnes told us, "Let's go, I want you all to stay together, and make sure you're all following me. We all need to hold each other's hands, do you hear me?"

As we walked up the main road, it was crowded with other Tutsis. Women, children, babies, men, elders, and their animals clogged the street, carrying as much as they could. Their baskets were stuffed with blankets and food. They carried mattresses, and some of the old men carried bottles of beer. Some of them looked like they had been walking all night, but everyone looked like they were leaving something behind, not knowing for sure if there would ever be a walk back home.

There were thousands of us walking toward Rwamagana Cathedral, and other government district offices, designated as safe zones. Auntie Agnes told us to continue walking with the other Tutsis, even though she didn't know where they were all going. She began asking some refugees where they were going, but most of them answered that they were just following the others. Auntie Agnes decided to do the same and hope for the best. Only a half a mile down the road from my grandparents' house, I heard whistles, and the faint strains of Hutu propaganda hate songs.

The sounds grew louder and without knowing exactly why, my heart began to race. Someone around me cried out, "The Interahamwe are coming to kill us!" An attack must have broken out right in front of where we were walking, for the people ahead of us bolted in a mass of confusion. Suddenly the street was full of killers, singing songs of hate, in the name of Jesus.

I lost my cousin's hand as a machete struck down a Tutsi immediately in front of me. Blood splattered across my face. Everywhere, whistles were blowing. In a split second I realized I was alone, and separated from my family. I was swept along with other people fleeing for their safety, and the next thing I knew, I was in the front yard of one of our Hutu neighbors. I looked down to find my beautiful white dress stained bright crimson with blood. I wasn't little Dydine anymore. My heart felt like it was going to explode. I looked around but my family was nowhere to be found.

Tutsi Refuges with their belongings 1994

Chapter Five: A Child of RPF Inkotanyi

The Interahamwe killers were terrible to look at, their faces distorted with rage. They were going to kill me for sure. I felt wet all over, and realized I was drenched in the blood of murdered Tutsis. People around me begged for forgiveness, though I didn't know what they had done wrong. I closed my eyes and was waiting for the machete to strike the back of my neck when somebody grabbed me.

Opening my eyes, I saw that I was standing in between a pair of legs. The owner of the pair of legs was an old man. The next thing I knew, he swept me up and carried me into a house with a bedroom with a small wooden bed, where other children were also hiding. He pushed me under the bed and held his fingers to his lips. The other children and I were silent, and although we were squeezed together so tightly, it felt like a luxury just to be there.

A minute later, I saw the old man's legs once again, as he crouched to pull me out from under the bed.

"You!" he said, pointing his finger right in my face. "You have to come with me. It's not safe for me to have you here inside my house, you are not like the other children. You're a child of the Inkotanyi.

"I have been waiting for darkness to fall so I can walk you to the hiding place." The old man was speaking out loud, but not quite directly to me, as though he were explaining himself to someone else. "I'm so sorry, dear, I cannot keep you here. If I do we're both going to get in trouble."

It was pitch black out, and so cold. We walked toward the banana plantation, on the path back to my grandparents' house. He brought me to a ditch, gently lowered me in, and put banana leaves around me. He told me to be silent. I wasn't to talk to anybody or respond to anybody but him. "Yes," he said, "I think this is the perfect place for you to stay, no one will think that you are here." Then he left and I was alone.

I was scared, but at least the banana leaves were warmer than wandering exposed in the darkness. I began to wonder whether everything that had happened was a terrible dream. Maybe I was still sleeping? Just then, raindrops began to plop and splatter against the banana leaves. I was definitely awake. The rain began lightly, and then grew into a furious downpour that began to flood the ditch.

I struggled to get free of the banana leaves and climb out, but I couldn't. The old man had barricaded the entrance to the ditch and I was too weak to break it open. I wasn't in danger of drowning, but the water was cold and I thought I might freeze to death if I couldn't break free.

I struggled and fought until I couldn't keep my anger inside of me any longer. I broke my promise and began to scream. I screamed and screamed until eventually I wore myself out and cried myself to sleep. When I woke, I had no idea how much time had passed. I waited in the freezing mud until finally the old man came back for me. He pulled me up from the ditch into the sunlight and gave me a sweet potato to eat.

"Hey!" he said. "Everything is going to be all right, I just don't want to see you killed, okay?"

He walked me towards my grandparents' house and told me again not to talk with anyone except for the people in my family. In what was once my house, there were now dozens of strangers, refugees who had fled from far away and had stopped here for shelter and food to eat. I didn't recognize anyone.

The man told me again, "Don't leave this place, ok? Wait for your family, ok Darling?" He began to back away. "Good luck, may God be with you," the old man said, and then he left. I was terrified to see him go. How could he leave me here, in this place that was at once so familiar and so strange? I crept quietly to a corner of the main room and tried to make myself as small as possible. Every little noise made me jump. I felt dirty and disgusting, my beautiful white dress with butterflies now unrecognizable, no white to be seen, only dirt and blood. I wished I had chosen another dress to wear for church.

I woke to the sound of Auntie Josephine's voice. She was arguing back and forth with Grandpa.

"No, I don't want to go anywhere," Grandpa said angrily. "I'll die inside my own house, as a man. I am not fleeing from those cowards!"

"Dad," Auntie Josephine pleaded. "The killers don't care if you're old or not, they will make you suffer. I can't leave you here alone. You must come with me!"

"I'm not changing my mind. I'm a dead man anyway, so just go and leave me. You have children to raise, Josephine."

I emerged from my hiding spot and followed the sound of their voices into the other room. The other refugees were still in the house, hiding quietly in every room. I walked on my tiptoes, not wanting to startle them, but then the dog Simba spotted me and ran into my arms, licking me and barking like mad.

"Dad, the Interahamwe are back!" Auntie Josephine said, her voice frantic. "We are dead!"

I was hugging Simba on the ground when I looked up to see Auntie Josephine's legs coming towards me. She dropped to her knees in front of me, tears filling her eyes. For a moment, we stared at each other, saying nothing. Auntie Josephine shook her head as though casting off a trance and held her arms wide open. I leapt into them.

"Dydine, Sweetheart!" Auntie Josephine lifted me up and looked around as though trying to figure out where I had come from or who I was with. Seeing that I was alone, she took me in to see my grandpa. I became like a petrified tree, numb, unable to express feelings anymore. I saw my grandpa lying in his bed. Drawing closer, I tried to give him a big hug as always, but he grimaced and pushed me away.

"Your grandpa is not feeling well, dear," Auntie Josephine said. "His whole body is hurting and he can't give hugs at the moment."

Listening to Auntie Josephine, I started walking backwards with my eyes fixed on Grandpa's. I realized everything and everyone had changed, and nothing would be like it was before.

I would later learn that Grandpa had been brutally beaten by the Interahamwe killers. They left him for dead, but when the rain fell upon him, Grandpa realized he was alive and crawled back to the house, which he vowed to never leave again. "My Madina," Grandpa said. "I'm so thrilled to see you right now, my beautiful Madina." I loved it when Grandpa called me Madina, it made me feel special. Grandpa looked at Auntie Josephine with a longing in his eyes, like he was asking her for something, but he didn't say a word. I realized he wanted her to take me away. He didn't want me to see him like this.

Auntie Josephine wrung her hands and looked up to the ceiling. "I cannot flee with Dydine and leave my dad alone, but I cannot leave Dydine here to die with us either. God, what should I do?" Auntie Josephine looked at me and asked,"Dydine, where is everyone else, how did you end up alone? Where is your Auntie Agnes and where are my children, your cousins?"

She picked me up and held me gently in her arms. I looked back at her quietly and said nothing. I was too scared to speak, and too tired to try to explain the answers to her questions, or to relive the awful moments of my recent memory. All I could do was stare at her and listen. Auntie Josephine took my silence to mean the worst.

"Dad, all my children are already dead," She said, tears rolling down her face. "I don't want to live anymore. What will my life be like without my children?"

Simba came in from outside, walking around all of us and nudging Auntie Josephine like he wanted to show her something. Someone was out there. My heart dropped with fear, as Auntie Josephine rushed to find a place to hide me. She turned one way, then another. She couldn't think straight.

"It's me!" came a whisper. "Everything is all right, don't be scared."

Auntie Agnes! We sighed with relief when we saw her.

"I'm here to pick up some blankets and see if anyone has survived. We should all go to Baringa's house...but I have bad news, I think Dydine did not make it, may her soul rest in peace. We have been separated since the first day of the nightmare. After a few seconds of absolute silence Auntie Josephine spoke, "Agnes, Dydine is here."

Auntie Agnes froze. When she saw me, she burst into tears and knelt down to hug me, cradling me close in her arms. I still felt numb, and although I wanted to, I couldn't show her any affection.

She started talking about her journey, speaking quickly as though once she started she could not stop. She told us how she survived and ran with baby Fils on her back, how she found herself chased by a group of Interahamwe killers, how she could not run fast enough to escape them with the added weight of the baby. When she was unable to run anymore, she thought about abandoning Fils, putting him down, so that she could save herself. She thought that there would be no way for them both to survive, so she decided to leave him on the ground and keep running.

Auntie Agnes said, "My heart kept telling me to go back to get him, but I kept trying to convince myself that I had made the right decision. I told myself that even Devota, who had given birth to this baby, left him for her own safety, and that justified me doing the same. I thought that we would die together if I kept him with me." She told us how Fils, the baby who could barely speak a word, called out to her by name,

"Agnes, don't leave me!"

She told us how when Fils called her by name, she felt like God was speaking to her.

Auntie Agnes said, "My heart froze in that moment, and I ran back to Fils and once again strapped him to my back, screaming,"If we die, we die together, if we survive, we gonna survive together! God will never forgive me if I leave you to die. "The killers were so close to us," Auntie Agnes said, "but somehow they saw other Tutsis running and decided to kill them first." Everyone was looking in Agnes's eyes, we all wanted to know what happened next.

"Running as fast as I could, we ran into Sebasaza. It seems impossible to believe but he rescued us!"

We were shocked. Sebasaza was our village recluse, a mean and grumpy old man with a hunchback.

"When I saw him right in front of me, I knew our deaths were in his hands, but on the contrary he said to me, "Your Dad was a good man, I will help you because of him."

Sebasaza took Auntie Agnes into his old, decrepit house. It was packed with Tutsis who were hiding from the Interahamwe, and it smelled terrible. Grandpa, Auntie Josephine and I were still in disbelief. Sebasaza? Really? Sebasaza, the man who couldn't say three words without swearing? All of us kids were afraid of him. Agnes joked about how she would tell us kids to go to school and not to complain or Sabasaza would come for a visit. The thought of this was so frightening that we would shut up and go to bed immediately without another word.

Looking back, it is ironic that he was one of the only people who had compassion for us Tutsis. I think the Interahamwe also knew of his reputation as a mean old man, and so they never thought to search his home. They would never have suspected he would do anything good for the Tutsis.

Auntie Agnes continued, "It wasn't long after we arrived at his house that Sebasaza started shouting at all of us, and we realized his generosity might not last long. I decided to escape with the kids. They're all there, in the plantation, waiting for me so we can go to Baringa's house. You're all coming with me, right?"

Grandpa said nothing and looked to Auntie Josephine, who busied herself fetching blankets. She changed me into clean clothes and a warm jacket.

Auntie Agnes pulled Auntie Josephine aside. "What shape is dad in?" she asked. "Why can't he get up?"

Auntie Josephine looked so sad then. She glanced at me and I pretended to play with the dog, like I wasn't listening.

"He was on the farm, just like every other day of his life, when the killings began, and he was attacked by Interahamwe killers. They tortured him, cut his finger, slaughtered and ate one of his cows, and abandoned him in the fields, thinking he was dead."

"Dad also thought he was dead. The night came and it started to rain. He opened his mouth and started drinking some of the water falling from the sky. He realized that he was still alive. He tried to crawl, and slid on his stomach on the ground trying to get back to the house in one piece. It took him all night, and he arrived the next morning." Josephine let out a heavy sigh.

"I have been telling him to flee with me, but he wants to die in his own bed at home. He won't listen to me, Agnes, but maybe he will listen to you." Agnes took my hand and started walking out the door. "Let's go. Dad, you know at Baringa's we can be safe. He is Hutu, but he is married to your sister in law. He must protect the family. Dad, please come with us!".

My grandfather spoke in a tired, low voice, "No, my dear, go take my grandchildren away and protect them. If they live, that is a blessing. I have seen a lot throughout my long life. I am an old man. I need my children's respect, please let me be. I want to die in my own house. Josephine, please go with them too and be with your children, they need you. I love you, you are wonderful daughters any father would have wished for. I have been a lucky man." He drew a shaky breath, and the effort seemed to pain him. "Please, if upon your return I am not still alive, give my love to whoever makes their way out of this massacre.

"Agnes," he gestured to my Auntie, and for the first time I noticed the blood stains seeping through clothe bandages that wrapped his fingers. "How are you going to get to Baringa's house without going through the Ikoni Center?

Don't tell me you are going to walk there with Mapuwa's kids. The kids of Inkotanyi!"

"We'll wait for the rain to come," Auntie Agnes replied. "I have heard the Hutu killers say that they do not work in the rain. If it is not our day to die, then we will be okay. She stood in the doorway and looked up to the sky. "God help me," Agnes said.

The Inkerahamwe killers with French troops who were the Hutu government supporters back then.

Chapter Six: No Tutsi God in My House

After the 1959 Revolution, unrest between the Hutus and Tutsis reached a boiling point. Once the Hutus overthrew the Rwandan monarchy, which was part of the Tutsi social class, the Hutus began to hunt the Tutsis. This was when my great grandfather was killed on Lake Muhazi. Shortly after, my great grandfather's 14-year-old daughter, Jane, was forced to marry a Hutu man named Baringa, to secure her safety and the safety of our family. It was to Jane and Baringa's house we were now headed for sanctuary.

My Auntie Josephine remained devoted to her father. Even after Grandpa's impassioned speech, she said goodbye to us and remained with him at the house. Once again, Auntie Agnes was the only adult leading all us kids to safety. We walked in the dark, the air cold and damp because it was the rainy season. I wished that I could hop into a warm bed and snuggle under my blanket, feeling its protection and comfort.

I was so tired of walking, but I kept placing one foot in front of the other. We walked to the plantation, where I had a brief but gleeful reunion with my cousins. Though we were still fleeing for our lives, the fact that I had survived thus far brought a smile to their sad faces. We hugged each other, and even in my cousins' embrace, I recall feeling numb. I didn't know what to feel anymore.

We waited for the rain to start so we could continue our journey. We knew that the Hutu extremists went inside to rest during periods of rain, and that it was the safest time to travel. As darkness descended we started to fall asleep, snuggling under all the blankets Auntie Agnes had brought for us. I woke abruptly to Auntie Agnes shaking my shoulder.

"Lets go now! It's raining! It's now or never!"

We quickly snuck out through the sorghum bushes and by the grace of God we made it all the way to Baringa's house. Baringa was the only Hutu man in the family that Agnes could think of. She truly believed he would protect us.

Auntie Agnes knocked timidly on the wooden door to his house. When Baringa answered the door, my eyes were level to his knees. He was a giant of a man. I looked up trying to see his face. Baringa scowled, annoyed, and once he realized why we had come he shut the door and cried out, "No, no, no! No more of you people! You best be leaving now!"

Auntie Agnes pleaded with Baringa, asking to take refuge just for one night so she could buy us some time and devise the next plan. They negotiated in whispers back and forth through the window. Just when Auntie Agnes started to give up, Jane opened the door and welcomed us in.

"Jane!" Baringa screamed. "Once I finish all this work outside, I'm going to start working inside, and don't think for one moment that I will allow all of these cockroaches inside my house!"

When Baringa mentioned, "Work," we knew what that meant-he meant kill. Jane tried to comfort us, saying, "Please ignore him, my husband has changed recently, I don't recognize him anymore." We walked into the living room. Tutsi children from everywhere were sitting there silently looking up at us. Jane started giving Auntie Agnes orders, whispering loudly so we all could hear her.

"Agnes, make the kids sit down here with the others. The younger ones in front and the older ones in the back. We need to be able to control them and keep them quiet because if any of Baringa's friends find out about us hiding Tutsis, they will burn the house down with all of us inside!"

I sat in the front row of that room for what felt like forever. I had lost all track of time. Later, I learned we remained at Baringa and Jane's for weeks. Somehow, Jane kept us safe. It was clear Baringa hated our presence, but he tolerated us. All I knew was that I would remain in the same spot until Auntie Agnes told me I could move. Agnes sat in the corner, where she could keep an eye on everyone. She held a strong stick in her hands, her face hardened, her expression warning us not to flinch.

We were told that if we coughed, or sneezed, we would be the first to be killed by the Interahamwe who were right outside the house. Just by being there, we were putting Baringa, Jane, and their children in danger. His wife was Tutsi and his children had Tutsi blood.

Dydine Umunyana

The Interahamwe were instructed to kill everyone who tried to help any Tutsi, or everyone who had some sort of Tutsi blood or connection. Auntie Agnes was like our own professional security guard. Whenever I looked at her, her eyes were open, watchful.

I was starving and tried to catch Auntie Agnes's eye to tell her how hungry I was, but she never looked directly at me. I think she was avoiding me on purpose. When our eyes finally did meet, my throat closed up and I couldn't talk. I started to cry. Auntie Agnes turned away, her gaze fixed resolutely on the wall. After a moment she turned around, looked me dead in the eye and said, "Dydine, what are you doing?"

I knew I wasn't allowed to cry, and I knew something bad might happen to me if I complained so I made up the first excuse I could think of.

"Uh, I don't know," I stammered. "Water just started falling all over my face..." Auntie Agnes heard this and she rolled her eyes, "Clean up your face right now, or else!"

I tried to do what she said, but I couldn't make the tears stop. When my gaze met Auntie Agnes's eyes, I saw she had tears in her eyes too. It was the first time I'd seen her cry.

That night, my baby brother Fils started screaming and wouldn't stop. He had been on Auntie Agnes's back since the start of this killing against Tutsis. I had never heard him scream this way, yet he was a baby and had no idea what was going on. Auntie Agnes tried to silence him by putting her hands over his little mouth, but it was impossible to soothe him. Baringa came rushing from his room with a fire torch in his hands. Shaking with anger, he yelled, "Leave my house right now! There is no God for Tutsis here in my house!"

It was almost 3 am when we began walking. The fog was so thick, it seemed like you could almost touch the darkness. I couldn't even see whose hands I was holding, but I knew we were all together in this. Agnes scanned the street, trying to spot any Interahamwe.

"Who is there?" A man called out into the darkness. It was Baringa's first son Sekamana, who heard us from the guesthouse where he was sleeping. He recognized Agnes and approached us. "Agnes, where are you going at this time? Go back into the house; it's not safe for you out here! You could be killed."

"Where do you want us to go back to?" Agnes asked. "Your father said there is no Tutsi God in his house and he is right, there sure isn't! We are leaving. Our Father in Heaven who has kept us alive until this day, he has been with us all along and we will make it out alive!"

As we continued walking, Sekamana called out again, "How do you think you are going to pass the Ikoni center? How will you survive it, Agnes? What you are doing is a suicide." Agnes held her head high and kept walking.

"Agnes, stop!" Sekamana yelled. "I'm coming with you."

Ikoni center was where all the Interahamwe in the village gathered to plan the killings on the Kucyamuvoma , and Sekamana believed he could protect us since he had Hutu blood, and was also a part of Interahamwe. He knew that it would take a miracle for us to survive. About a hundred feet from Ikoni center, I heard a whisper coming from a nearby bush. Dread washed over me. We all stopped moving.

A grown woman emerged from the bushes, holding her hands up in surrender. "It's me, Mugenzi's wife. Please, Agnes, help me, I haven't killed any Tutsis!" She was a Hutu woman, one whom I had seen before. I thought perhaps she was Auntie Josephine's neighbor.

"Don't shout! Agnes answered. "What are you afraid of, your husband is one of the Interahamwe. I am here with all these damn kids! We're the ones who are supposed to be begging for your help! Keep your voice down so your husband doesn't come to kill us all!"

Mugenzi's wife responded, "You don't know the news. Things have changed, and the RPF Inkotanyi (Rwanda Patriotic Front) have arrived and now are fighting for justice against the perpetrators. The Interahamwe have fled. Please help me and tell them I'm not one of the Interahamwe killers!" Immediately, Auntie Agnes told Sekamana to return home. We continued to walk into the night without him, now on our way back to my grandparents' house. It took all night. I don't remember ever having traveled so far.

I had a strange sensation somewhere between being starving and being sick. We hadn't eaten for days, yet as we walked the stench of dead bodies filled our nostrils and made us retch on the side of the road. I realized the fog was not just morning humidity; there were ashes everywhere. Not even the birds that normally sang were calling out to each other. There were no cars on the road, and everything felt so empty. Auntie Agnes picked up the pace, trying to walk faster so that we could get home before sunrise, or before anybody saw us, because she wasn't sure what was true and what was false anymore, or who was safe, and who was not. I realized there was nothing more Auntie Agnes could do to protect us. Now, we truly were in God's hands.

We were almost past the Ikoni center, when out of the darkness a huge angry turkey charged towards us. We screamed and ran like the Interahamwe were after us. Some of my cousins actually believed it was the Interahamwe. Luckily, this only made us run faster, and we arrived close to my grandparents' house just as the sun was rising. A loud boom rang out as we approached the front yard. Gun fire.

"From now on, if you hear anything loud, you have to get down on the ground immediately!" Auntie Agnes commanded us. It started to feel like a game, walking a little bit, getting down on the ground, getting back up only to walk a few feet, and hustling to get back down to the earth once again. We were almost to the house, we'd almost made it, and yet, there was danger everywhere.

The Interahamwe killers with their weapons in 1994

Chapter Seven: The Bloody Center

When we arrived at my grandparents' house, Auntie Josephine heard us and came out. She was shocked when she saw the condition we were in. I think she must have thought we are ghosts. With a big smile and tears flowing down her face, she ran towards us.

"There is no more fear!" she cried. "You don't have to be scared. Things have changed. We are not going to die anymore! The RPF Inkotanyi soldiers are everywhere. They are our guides now. They are here in the field. We can speak out loud! We are free!"

It was more words than I'd ever heard Auntie Josephine say at one time. She began to tell us the story of how she had survived. During the day she would go and hide in the banana plantation, and during the night or during the rain she would come back to check in on Grandpa. The Interahamwe would come to the house once a day intending to finish him off, but Grandpa was smart, and he knew he had something they wanted. He would bribe them with the leftovers from Grandama's banana beer production business, which amused the Interahamwe and kept them drunk and happy.

They would leave Grandpa with the same old promise, that tomorrow they would come back to the house and kill him. "You old man, we will kill you tomorrow, don't forget to pray for your soul!" they would say. The same thing happened day after day, and they would not tell another Interahamwe their secret and always made the same promise to him, but as long as Grandpa produced the banana beer, he knew he had a chance at staying alive. Grandpa and Auntie Josephine thought they were the only Tutsis that had survived, until now.

Auntie Agnes could barely speak. Reunited with her sister and father, she seemed to finally let her guard down, and the trauma of the last few weeks, which she had not permitted herself to think about until now, set in.

She managed to mumble a few words to Auntie Josephine. "I want water please."

"Oh yes, of course," Auntie Josephine exclaimed. "Let me get you something to drink, I can even get you something to eat! Let me go pick some bananas from the yard and cook you all up a plate. We have a lot to catch up on. I have some good news; the kids' father came back into our lives last night. Two young men in uniforms came to our house, they asked for Dydine and her brother..."

"I hope you said that you don't know them..." Auntie Agnes said.

"Let me finish," Auntie Josephine continued. "I trembled and begged them to kill me with a gun, and not a machete. I told them, "Please, my children! Don't make me suffer. You can take anything that I have, take everything! I don't have money, but you can have my house! Take the beans, and the food inside! You can have anything you want but please don't cut me to death with the machete! If I'm going to die, I want to die immediately."

"Then I jumped up and took the gun from them, but I had no idea how to use it. If I knew, I think I would have shot myself right then. But my day was not yet to come. They kept insisting I tell them about Dydine and her little brother. They told me they were not Interahamwe. I didn't understand. I was so terrified, I kept telling them just to shoot me, and to finish me off. They tried to calm me down saying....

"Our mother, please listen to us, we are not killers, we have come here to help you! Laurent, Dydine and Fils' father, is our commander. He has sent us here to see if his kids are still alive. Please tell us, and stop this nonsense. We don't have time for this! We have a country to save! Our brothers and sisters are dying and we came to stop the Hutu Interahamwe extremists!'"

All Auntie Josephine could do was look in their eyes. She could not breathe, but finally she spoke again. "I know where the kids are and they are still alive. I can take you to them now!" When the men in uniform heard this news they just said thank you, and promised that they would come back later the following day. They told Auntie Josephine to pack everything important and to get ready to leave. She couldn't believe we had showed up on the very same day the men in uniforms were supposed to return. It was a miracle and she was very excited. "I'm going to cook something to eat!" she said, and off she went.

None of us had ever seen Auntie Josephine so animated and worked up. It was unusual for her to be so giddy. She was known around town as not being very helpful when it came to remembering details about important events. Even if she did know what happened, she had a hard time expressing herself. She was usually the observer of a conversation, not the center of it.

My cousins and I all looked at each other, dumbfounded. For a moment we forgot about all the pain and suffering we had just experienced, and started laughing. We doubled over with laughter; it was just too funny to see Auntie Josephine this way. Suddenly, I felt exhausted and overwhelmed. I don't know what hit me, but as soon as Auntie Josephine went in the kitchen to start cooking, I became dizzy. I smelled the memories from meals past as the scent of cooked bananas entered the room. It was so powerful, it knocked me out.

I must have lost consciousness, because the next thing I remember I was on the floor looking up at Agnes, who was touching my face with a wet towel and handing me a glass of water. I had fainted. I was gone for a while and then came back to life. They tried to ask me what was wrong, but because I had never had this problem before, I didn't know what to say. I just looked around at them, my eyes wide and my mouth shut.

While Auntie Josephine continued preparing the food for us, the sound of men singing came from over the surrounding hill. The sound grew louder, it was coming right towards us. I recognized the Interahamwe hate songs from the first morning of the attacks. Now they sang about how they had finished off the neighbors who lived behind the hill next door, and they were coming to see who was left in our village.

There was no longer a time to stop, to eat, or even take a breath, the chase was on again. The empty street we had just walked along filled with people. They came out of nowhere, out of hiding in the bush, or perhaps they had been walking for days. Auntie Agnes knew that it was time to flee yet again and we began following these people. The killers ran down the hill towards us. If we didn't run fast enough, we knew we would be slaughtered. Auntie Josephine and Auntie Agnes organized all of us so quickly. Auntie Agnes put Fils on her back as usual, and told me to follow her close. Auntie Josephine stayed with Grandpa.

We walked for miles. Some people had been walking for days. A few dropped dead from hunger and thirst, others were trampled because they couldn't keep up and were exhausted, their skin infected and bleeding from machete wounds. We were headed to Uganda, but only by the grace of God would we make it there. We had nothing left except our prayers. I asked God in every spare moment for us to live to see the following day. On the way to Uganda, Auntie Agnes saw a man walking towards us and she stopped walking when she recognized him.

It was my father Laurent. He had been on his motorcycle, searching for us. I couldn't believe I was finally meeting him. He was of average height with dark skin and a regal bearing. I thought he was very handsome and felt proud he was my father. He greeted Auntie Agnes quickly and asked her to give him his children. Auntie Agnes took Fils from her back and handed him to Laurent, but my little brother cried so hard because he had never met our father. Then Agnes told Laurent to take me instead of Fils since he was having such a fit.

Then my father begged me to go with him. Though he was my father, I had never met him before and he was still a strange man to me. But I knew I had no choice and had to do what Agnes told me. Even though I was separating from my brother, Auntie, and cousins, I accepted.

Laurent my new found father picked me up, put me on the back of his motorcycle, and told me to hold on tight to his body. We drove back to Rwamagana City where RPF Inkotanyi soldiers had already gained control of Eastern Province. On our way to the army camp, I started vomiting violently because I couldn't stand the stench of the burning houses mixed with the heavy stench of dead bodies decomposing in the streets. I was four years old and we were in the final days of May 1994, but the genocide was not yet over. Our entire country was on fire.

My father received a call from his high commanders to go to work, which meant rescuing the Tutsis who had survived, and he had no other choice but to leave me at the camp with the other RPF Inkotanyi soldiers. He told them to feed me and keep an eye on me. I knew I had to remain calm. Everyone around me was in uniform, which intimidated me but also made me feel safe. I didn't want to talk to anyone, especially now that Dad had left me, so I walked by myself to find a place to sit alone. I felt like the whole world had abandoned me. In my mind all I could remember was the look Auntie Agnes gave me before we had parted ways, as if she were warning me to do as I was told and not cause any trouble. I knew I should just try to accept whatever would come next.

I observed the soldiers. Everyone was doing different things. Some were playing, laughing, fighting, crying loudly, cooking, having a drink, smiling. It was a mixture of activities and myriad emotions. A group of RPF Inkotanyi soldiers came up to me, trying to be funny and engage me in childish games. I knew they were trying to make me smile, but this was the last thing I wanted to do. All I wanted was to go back to my family; they were the only ones who could make me smile now. The soldiers eventually backed away, concerned.

Auntie Agnes had raised us not to accept food from strangers. Even though I was starving, and even though the soldiers were trying to feed me, because I didn't know any of them, I refused to eat. Towards the end of the night a few soldiers sat right next to me, and watched over me, waiting for me to fall asleep. But I could not close my eyes. The hours ticked by until most of the soldiers dozed off but I stayed up. Even though they had made me a little mattress to sleep on, I didn't feel tired at all. My heart started racing and didn't stop until my dad returned to camp. He took me to bathe, and when I was finished he told me,

"I have something for you, guess what it is?" I just looked up at him without saying anything at all.

"Is everything all right, little Dydine?" he asked.

He put a clean dress on me. When I looked down, I saw a beautiful white dress with three little butterflies, exactly like the one Grandpa gave me for Christmas! I looked up at my dad and smiled, and one of the soldiers looked at me and said, "You actually are beautiful!" He thought he was being funny. My dad told me to ignore him and asked me if I wanted milk. Again, since my dad was strange to me, I refused. Eventually, I accepted it, to be polite, but I put it on the ground and knocked it over "on accident" as I walked towards my mattress to sleep. I fell into a very deep sleep.

When I woke up I was once again with Auntie Agnes and all the other kids. I struggled to make sense of my surroundings. My father had realized he could not be both a father and a soldier of war at the same time. He was needed to rescue other Tutsis and couldn't continue leaving me every day while he worked. He decided the best thing he could do was return me to the family I knew. He also knew I would have died if I kept refusing food.

My father must have assumed he was leaving me in a safe place, but I awoke to a war zone. I was back in the middle of nowhere, amongst thousands of people running, crying, walking, hugging. It was very disorienting, and the overall effect made me feel more numb than ever. Bullets whizzed by and grenades exploded all around us. We were inside a tiny structure that didn't even have a door. It looked like it was part of an abandoned shopping center, In Kayonza one of the Kibungo districts. Everything was falling apart.

We saw many people die that day. I felt we were moments away from meeting death ourselves. By this time, we had stopped praying. In the camp someone started singing a gospel song, one that was familiar to me because we sang it in church. Those of us who were still alive joined in chorus. We had nothing, but we found strength in this music. When all other faith was lost, this made us smile. All we wanted was to enjoy our last moment.

Children of God be strong,

Persevere and keep your eyes open

Always be ready,

Because the Lord is coming back for us

The time is now to go to heaven,

Ask for mercy from God,

for all your sins can be washed away in the

blood of Jesus Christ.

The singing grew louder than the sound of death and bombs. Death had become familiar to us, and none of us could see how we would survive this moment.

Suddenly, a convoy of RPF Inkotanyi soldiers arrived with trucks to move all of us refugees to Nyagatare near Muhazi Lake, another city in the Eastern Province. Laurent had made sure to send a truck especially for my cousins, my Auntie, my brother and me. As the truck arrived. I couldn't believe my eyes! Grandpa and Josephine were sitting in the back of the truck. Somehow, they were still alive! The RPF Inkotanyi soldiers packed as many people into the truck as would fit, and began to drive toward the Ugandan border. As we rode along, the chorus of that song kept replaying in my mind, and I started humming it softly.

Once again, everyone started singing along with me, but this time we sang in gratitude and relief. It was about an hour's drive to safety in near Ugandan boarders. We got to the small city of Nyagatare in the Eastern Province, where the RPF Inkotanyi soldiers stopped to loot an abandoned hospital. They brought us medicine, bandages, mattresses, and other medical supplies. We remained here until we heard the good news: the killing had ended in the eastern Province but was still going on in other parts of the country.

President Paul Kagame, who headed to RPF Inkotanyi back then in early 1990s', my mom found this photos in the hands of one of the Genocide victims.

Chapter Eight: An Unexpected Reunion

The surviving refugees, including my family and me, took shelter inside the hospital near the Ugandan border. We spent all our time gathered together indoors, afraid to leave the hospital grounds. The country's atmosphere was still toxic, and no one knew what was happening in the streets. After all that had occurred, it seemed impossible that Tutsis and Hutus could return to living peaceably side-by-side.

The confinement was hardest on us children. We weren't used to being kept indoors and in spite of all we had seen; we didn't understand the weight of the situation. I was naïve. I went outside, like I always did. I just wanted to get some fresh air. I stood beside the road for a while, observing the beauty of the countryside and probably thinking how at odds it was with our man-made chaos. Buses passed by belonging to the RPF Inkotanyi, full of soldiers singing songs of courage and victory. Amidst the busses, I spotted an old, small green pickup truck, its back filled with women and men in uniform.

A strange woman from their group looked at me from the truck, and in an instant she jumped from the truck and began running towards me. The truck was still driving away as she approached.

"Hey! What the hell are you doing, soldier?" another soldier yelled from the back of the truck.

"Stop the car!" the woman yelled back, tears streaming down her face. "My daughter!" she exclaimed.

"You have a daughter?" the soldier replied.

She was still running. "And a son!" When she reached me, the woman hugged me so tight I could scarcely breathe. I could see from over her shoulder that the other soldiers were shocked and didn't know what to do. I was so afraid. The woman was crying so loudly, and I had no idea who she was.

She claimed to be my mother, but I told myself it was not possible. This is not what I imagined my mother would look like. I thought my mother was a monster. We'd been told by the media, the politicians, our neighbors, everyone, that the RPF Inkotanyi soldiers were snakes with horns, long ears and a long tail, but this woman was beautiful!

"It's me, I'm your mom," she kept repeating through her tears. I was so confused I started crying too. She kept holding me and I couldn't break free from her embrace. My cries turn to screams, which got the attention of somebody who came to help me. Everyone from inside the hospital shelter came out to see what all the commotion was about.

"Mapuwa!" someone screamed. They recognized Devota immediately.

Everyone embraced, crying tears of joy, then they peppered her with a million questions about how she had survived, and who had died. They wanted to know everything. Half of my Aunties and uncles had already been killed, but no one had heard anything about Grandma. We assumed she had also been killed but no one knew for sure. The morning the killings began, she had been traveling to Kigali to sell her banana beer. No one had heard anything from her since then.

We all sat around and watched my mom like she had been dead this whole time and had just now come back to us from the afterlife. A soldier came in to tell my mother that they had to keep moving. "I have to go," she told us, "but don't worry, I will be back before you know it." She hugged and kissed my brother and me, and walked away with the soldiers. We watched her leaving again, with tears in our eyes as we waved goodbye.

My mother kept her promise. That same day she came back to us with food and clothes.

"I couldn't live another day without my children," she said. She asked Auntie Agnes if she could take Fils and me with her. Agnes agreed but my little brother refused to go.

He didn't know my mom at all, and Auntie Agnes had been his only caretaker for as long as he could remember. If it was difficult for Auntie Agnes to part with Fils, and me but she put on a brave front. She told my mom to take my cousin Kadafi with her. Kadafi was Mignone's younger brother, and almost two years older than I was.

Fils loved Kadafi so much, we suspected he would be all right with my mother as long as Kadafi was nearby. Later that night we left the others and moved away with my mom. I didn't know where we were going. I was so tired, I slept the entire car ride.

When I woke up it was morning and we were inside a beautiful house. I was frightened and disoriented, but Kadafi's presence comforted me. We decided to sneak outside to explore. We knew we had traveled far, and that we were now under a new sky. It turned out to be an RPF Inkotanyi training center in Cyondo, also close to the Ugandan border. We saw soldiers doing their morning running, and others carrying heavy objects to build their strength. There were a lot of other kids there too, sitting silently in a sad loneliness.

While wandering around the camp, we saw a little tin shed house. We went in and found bullet shells and picked them up thinking they were toys. Excitedly Kadafi and I sat down and started playing with them, throwing them at each other. Next to us were three stones bordering hot embers of the cooking fire from the night before. Several of the shells accidentally fell in the middle of the stones. And it sounding like gun shots.

"Dydine!" someone shouted. It was my mother, Devota. She was furious. She ran out to me and grabbed my arm, whirling me around. "Never leave the house without my permission! You must always tell me where you're going. These are the rules. Do you understand?"

Dydine Umunyana

We turned and walked slowly back to the house. I couldn't help glancing back over my shoulder. I couldn't stop gazing at this beautiful place, and I couldn't get the image of those lonely children out of my mind. Where were their parents, I wondered? Had they died in the attacks? As we approached the house, I heard Fils screaming from inside. He'd been crying nonstop since we arrived at the training camp, and he was making my mom crazy. On the second day, my mother took Fils back to Agnes. I was confused by Fils's disappearance, but at least Kadafi remained with me at the camp. Mom's soldier girl friends watched over us and took care of us. Mom was one of the few women in RPF Inkotanyi who had children. Her friends seemed to think it was fun to have us around.

For weeks my mom would come and go, but somehow whenever she returned, she managed to bring back good news. One day she returned to tell me that they had found my Grandma Madeline. It was a miracle she was still alive, but she was in bad shape. I asked my mother to tell me how she'd survived. She raised an eyebrow and looked me up and down, as if assessing whether I was able handle the truth. She decided I could. I was not even quite 5 years old.

Grandma had already made it to the market in Kigali when the attacks began, she told me. The Interahamwe swarmed the market where she was selling her banana beer. No one had time to run or hide. They were surrounded. The Interahamwe started killing Tutsis one by one. They made everyone show their ID cards just to be sure they got them all. Grandma was struck by a machete on her arm and leg, and she fell into a pile of dead bodies. She thought she was already dead, but hours went by and she felt drops of water being poured on her mouth. This is when she realized she was still alive. When she opened her eyes, she saw a young girl standing over her with a water jug. The girl told Grandma that she was sorry she could not carry her, but she wanted to stay and help her. She refused to leave my grandmother alone.

The little girl told Grandma that she also had been close to death but the angels refused to take her too. She waited with Grandma for days until the RPF Inkotanyi arrived, and she raced to the soldiers, telling them there was someone still breathing! They took Grandma to an emergency room in parliament house where they treated her wounds immediately. It was exciting news to hear that Grandma was still alive. I couldn't wait to see her again.

Another time, my mom came back with news that she'd found my father in Ruhengeri, and that they had made plans to reunite our family. My father had gone to Ruhengeri to rescue his family, but by the time he'd arrived, it was already too late. My grandmother's premonition had been realized. My father's entire family had been killed nearly four months earlier, by Hutu neighbors on the first day of the killings. When my dad arrived, his home was unrecognizable. The Hutus had burned all the houses in his neighborhood and transformed the land into a potato and maize plantation.

The whole world stood still and did nothing to prevent the killings. No one could explain what had happened to so many Tutsi civilians in only one hundred days. Some people called it the apocalypse. This act was committed by Rwandans killing other Rwandans, and it was stopped by Rwandans, this ethnic massacre nobody could name, categorize or explain. It wasn't until months later, we learned a new word.

Genocide. noun

"Mass murder, mass homicide, massacre; annihilation, extermination, elimination, liquidation, eradication, decimation, butchery, bloodletting; pogrom, ethnic cleansing, holocaust."

Chapter Nine: Inside the Silent War

The entire country had been destroyed. A million people had been killed, entire villages had burned, and the country was in ashes. Those who had survived were in pain, not only physical but psychological. There was no time for families to grieve. No time to commemorate the dead or bury their bodies.

As we collectively emerged from our shock, a devastating loneliness set in. Our lives were unrecognizable from what they had been before. We grieved for the dead, and we grieved for an entire way of life that was gone. We were ourselves, and yet we were not. I was still a child, and yet I was not. I had seen things that no one would wish for any child or anyone to see.

It would be many years before true healing could begin, both for me and for my country. No one had time to sit still and reflect. The Interahamwe had now either been captured or had escaped the country, never to be seen again. Some Hutus who were innocent and who had not committed any crime also fled Rwanda in confusion. Meanwhile, Tutsis who had been living in exile for more than three decades began to return to their home country Rwanda after the RPF Inkotanyi's victory. The country was a mess.

Perhaps somewhat surprisingly, it was only after the genocide that my family seized its first real chance at togetherness. The world around me may have been in ruins, but I was strangely hopeful. I was looking forward to living with both my parents for the very first time. We were moving to the northern province of Rwanda in Ruhengeri, where my father was from, and I thought Fils and I might now experience the kind of familial love and happiness we'd never had before.

Mom emerged to have me start school the first morning we arrived in Ruhengeri. But it did not last as my mother had wished; there was a terrorist attack on our school. The Interahamwe killers and former Hutu government Militias who had fled Rwanda after the genocide, now called Abacengezi, frequently returned to Rwanda killing people who had survived. Our School was called Nyamagumba and it was both kindergarten and primary school. We were hundreds of students. The youngest were 3, the oldest were 12 and I was 5. While studying in my new class, we heard gun shots and grenades. I knew that sound and I knew what comes with it. Death!

Running as fast as I could, I forgot my way home. Flashbacks playing in my head, I found my self sitting in a strange store, covering my ears and burying my head between my legs. Hours passed until my mother and father found me in that store. They had heard the news and had been searching for me desperately. They took me back home.

That first night I spent under the same roof with both my parents, I fell asleep with a smile on my face. I snuggled under the covers, feeling warm and safe. I woke up in the darkness to the sound of voices screaming, and I thought I was dreaming of the killings again.

"Please don't kill my children, please don't make my children orphans!"

The voice sounded like my mother's. With a chill shivering down my spine, I realized it was no dream. My mother was screaming from her room.

"They are the only family that I have left!"

I climbed out of bed and followed the sounds to my parents' room. The door was ajar and I peered inside. What I saw took my breath away.

My mother lay on the floor, crying, as my father stood over her, pressing down on her head with his army boot. The man I saw was unrecognizable from the person I met months ago who gave me a nice bath and my beautiful white dress. His eyes were red, and his face was twisted. I couldn't believe what I was seeing. My dad put more weight on my mother's head, making it hard for her to scream or even breathe.

I was frozen as I watched them, trying to understand what was happening. My dad looked up and noticed me spying on them through the door opening. He raised his arm, and I saw he was clutching a gun. He pointed it right at me and fired. My mother screamed and somehow found the strength to push my dad away. She ran to me, accidentally knocking us both over. I was so scared I couldn't think.

"Mama!" I cried.

She grabbed me and ran into my bedroom to get Fils, and together we fled from the house with my father fast behind us.

"We should not live!" he screamed, chasing us out the front door. "We should die, there is no point in living. I don't want my children to die horribly from machetes. I can't let the Interahamwe murder my children in front of me."

I was confused. My father had protected us from the Interahamwe. He'd told us they wouldn't harm us anymore. This was the first time I saw a man's tears, and the sight unnerved me. In our culture, men were supposed to be stronger than the rest of us, but I realized in that moment that my father was no longer in control. Luckily, his bullet missed me and we were able to get away unscathed. Scared by the gunshot, Fils cried louder than I'd ever heard him. And so began our new journey of running, yet again.

I will never forget the sound of my mother's voice later that night, as we hid outside in the darkness, still afraid to return home, when she told me,

"Dad will be fine, Dydine. He is going to be ok! He loves us so much. He is just not doing well right now, okay, Sweetie?" Through her tone of false cheerfulness, I heard the fear in her voice. She was begging me, a child, to be compassionate towards my father. She was also trying to reassure herself.

We slept outside the rest of the night and early in the morning we walked back to the house so we wouldn't be seen. We arrived at the same time as a group of soldiers, who had come to arrest my father. One of our neighbors had heard the gunshot, certain my father was teaching my mother how to shoot a gun illegally. The soldiers took my father away. I didn't know when we would see him again, or whether his absence would be a blessing or a curse.

I try now to imagine what my dad was feeling that night. It was all so confusing to me then, and it is still difficult to understand. He was so gentle and loving during the day, but at night he was a different person. PTSD or Post Traumatic Stress Disorder was not something many people in my country knew of then. Instead we talked of trauma. My father had been "traumatized" by the Genocide. He'd learned that nobody in his family had survived. Everyone was murdered, and their deaths were brutal and bloody. His home no longer existed. He'd returned to Ruhengeri to save his family, but he had failed. It seemed reason enough for a person to go mad, although my mother insisted it wasn't madness and that he was getting better, that being back with his family would make him better.

Even with my father away in prison, my life became a nightmare in which there was no escape, no peace. A full night's sleep became an unimaginable luxury. Another war was waging, a silent one, inside my own head. On the evenings I managed to sleep, I was haunted by terrible nightmares. In my dreams, I saw people being slaughtered. They were always people I knew. My brother, my Aunties, my parents and grandparents. I'd wake up screaming, thinking I was the only one left on the planet.

My mother didn't understand what was wrong with me. My dad had been able to tell her his story of survival, but I still had never been able to tell my mother mine, because I was still putting together all the pieces of the truth, of actual reality. Somehow, it resurfaced, in nightmares, and flashbacks. During those days in Ruhengeri, I walked around so terrified all the time that I couldn't bear to relive any of it. I held my fear inside, pushed it down and tried to escape my memories. Every time that I woke up from a nightmare the first thing I saw was my mom's concerned face, trying to comfort me.

All I could think to say was, "Why?"

My mother made up an old story, the Story of Keza, which means "beauty," to try to explain what was happening in our lives. Her voice was soothing and beautiful, and I quieted under the spell of her words.

Once open a time, there was a beautiful little village called Muhazi. Muhazi was a happy place. The children ran through the streets, laughing, playing and dancing, and their parents held parties and ceremonies every night. Muhazi was a happy place, except for one family, a family of outcasts. They were a mother and daughter, and they were never invited to any ceremonies or weddings. The family was poor and lonely, and no one cared.

When the other children played, the daughter stayed behind and watched. She was never invited to join in the fun. At every opportunity the family was excluded and marginalized. The daughter wondered why—what had they done to be so miserable? She asked her mother where her father was, wondering whether things would be different if he were around, but her mother never answered. As she grew up, she repeated the same question time and time again: where is my father?

One day, her mother finally broke down and revealed her secret. Dear Keza, she said, your father is alive and well. He left to join the kingdom's army when you were born. He loved you and he loved me but now we will never see him again and we must accept this. Because you don't have a brother, and because you are a girl, you cannot take his place in the army, and so he can never leave. So you see, our family is cursed. Without a man to lead our house, we will never be invited anywhere.

The daughter listened without saying a word. Then and there, she decided she would be the boy to take her father's place. A few days later, she disguised herself as a boy and joined the kingdom's army. She worked hard and improved her skills every day. Eventually she became well known as a fighter and a hero. But one day someone found out her secret and the news that a girl had tricked the kingdom's army traveled all the way to the king.

The king was outraged that he'd been made to look like such a fool, and he organized a ceremony to kill the daughter. As the day of her death arrived, the daughter presented herself to the king proudly. Although she faced death, she was filled with joy, because her mission had succeeded. Because she had taken his place, her father had been allowed to return home.

When the king saw her face, he recognized her as the great hero. Stunned, he exclaimed for all to listen, "Oh, this is the person? The strongest fighter I have? If all women can serve the kingdom as you have done, I want an army of women to defend my kingdom. And so the kingdom recruited women and Keza became the head of the army of Rwanda.

I loved the story, even as I knew it wasn't real. Even so, my mother's voice and strong arms comforted me, and eventually I was able to go back to sleep. Little did my family know, the worst was yet to come.

My Mom Devota in late 1990's

Chapter Ten: Help me Cry

Ultimately, it was decided my mother would move to Kigali with me and Fils, but our father would stay behind temporarily in Ruhengeri in prison.

"Please don't you worry," she told us. "Your father will meet us in our new home once he finishes up work."

I wasn't worried. As far as I was concerned, the longer we were separated, the better. I wanted to love my father, as my mother told me I should, but I couldn't reconcile his two faces; the kind, gentle man he was during the day and the tortured, violent man he was at night. When I thought of my father, the emotion that overwhelmed all others was fear.

My family and I began a very long journey. My mother urged my father to leave Ruhengeri and move to Kigali, a city about two hours southeast. She thought it would help him to be far from his home, where he wouldn't be reminded of his family and the murders all the time. She didn't know anything about PTSD; none of us did.

No one spoke of my father's "episodes" outside the family. My mother stressed that it was very important we keep his sickness secret, to preserve the pride of the family name. Life was miserable for me and my brother Fils, but we accepted the reality that we simply had to deal with it. We thought we were normal. We though every family was just like ours.

We arrived in our new home in Kigali, which was an empty house mom found for us. Auntie Josephine was waiting for us and had prepared a nice meal for us our first evening there. The trepidation I'd felt as we reached our new home, this time in a large army truck piled sky high with our belongings, disappeared as Auntie swept me up in a soft warm hug.

My mom seemed grateful for Auntie Josephine's efforts, but at dinner she was so tired I caught her swaying in her chair. She picked at her food, then dropped her fork. The room grew quiet and we stared at each other before mom jumped up and ran to her room, with Josephine close behind her. Fils and I made eye contact across the table. His face remained impassive, but I knew he was scared. His eyes questioned mine. *What's happening?* It was beginning to seem as though we could read each other's minds. No one understood me like Fils. It often felt like he was my only ally.

We listened to my mother cry and vomit from within her room. We later learned she was pregnant. We would have a sibling. After discovering her pregnancy, my mother doubled her efforts to bring my father back to Kigali. She began traveling back and forth to Ruhengeri, often leaving us alone at night. Each time she returned without my father, she seemed more angry. We did silly dances and told her jokes, trying to make her laugh, but it was rare even to be able to make her smile.

One night she returned to our house after an especially long trip to Ruhengeri. She knocked at the door and when we opened it, she was smiling.

"Guess who is here?" she said.

We stared at her without responding, unsure what to make of her upbeat attitude. It wasn't like her to be so cheerful, and we were suspicious. Fils and I had grown wary of surprises. She gave up waiting for us to answer. "It's your Dad!" she exclaimed, stepping aside for him to enter. My mother had been able to prove my father's innocence and he had been released from prison. Because he was a high-ranking soldier, it had not been difficult to convince the authorities to let him go.

My dad walked in with a sad expression, his eyes downcast as though he were ashamed. He gave each of us a weak hug and went to bed right away. We watched him disappear down the hall to his room and close the door. We were briefly optimistic that he might have recovered from his sickness, but soon it became apparent my father could not accept the reality of what had happened to his family. Late at night, Fils and I heard him and my mother quarreling. We listened, breathless, waiting for the conversation to spill into violence.

"I'm a failure!" Dad yelled.

"There was nothing you could have done, Laurent," my mother said. "No one could have saved them."

"I only joined the RPF Inkotanyi to rescue my family, and it got me nowhere. It nearly cost me you and the children. I failed everyone."

"It is time to look forward," my mother said. "We have a new life together now."

"There is no life after this mass killing," my dad said softly. He sounded like a very old man, as though all the energy had left him. "Sometimes I wish I'd never survived. When I close my eyes at night, I dream the Interahamwe are here. I see them raise their machetes to kill my children. My only comfort is the thought that I can take my gun and kill us quickly, before they hack us to death."

I was puzzled by my father's dark dreams. Why did he want us to die, I wondered, when we all had fought so hard to live? It was something of a miracle in those days in Rwanda to have an intact family. Most children I knew were missing a parent, a sibling, or were orphaned. By everyone else's standards, we were the lucky ones. Even with my father's rages, it was hard to feel sorry for ourselves when so many others around us had lost so much more.

One night, Fils and I lay awake in our room, our ears attuned for any movements in the house like we always did.

"What's wrong with him?," Fils whispered from his bed. "He's different."

"Nothing's ever right with him," I said.

Dad kept to his bed for weeks until he felt ready to leave the house. He didn't seem physically ill, just so dispirited he couldn't bring himself to get up. Since he had returned with my mother, we hadn't seen much of him. My mother brought him trays of food in his room. Fils and I tiptoed around the house, afraid to laugh or raise our voices. Something was wrong, we knew, but whatever it was, it was better than how things had been before. We didn't want to make a false move that might upset the equilibrium. We didn't want to trigger the nighttime beatings again.

When dad finally left the house, we heaved a collective sigh of relief. We could breathe again. We didn't have to be so nervous. Fils and I smiled at each other across the table as we ate our breakfast. Fils had inherited our mother's storytelling ability and liked to re-tell movie plot lines he'd hear about from the other kids in the neighborhood. He launched into a story about an elaborate car chase, and it was so good to see him animated and energized again. I realized I felt happy, for the first time in weeks. I wished my dad would stay out all day.

As it turned out, I got my wish, but we paid a heavy price. There was no sign of my dad in the early evening, and we ate a silent dinner without him. I could tell my mother was growing anxious. She kept glancing at the door, or running to the window, thinking she heard him coming down the street. In the end, we heard him long before we saw him.

Some kind of skirmish was happening in the road. Several voices rose, one of them my father's, and a woman screamed. We sprang to the window to see my dad stumbling down the road, accosting everyone he met. He swung wildly at each person he encountered, some punches landing on unfortunate passers by, others missing by a mile and throwing him off balance. He was trailed by a group of soldiers who seemed reluctant to intervene. I realized they were scared of him too. My stomach sank as I realized they were escorting him home, nothing more. They were more interested in protecting my father than in protecting us.

All the lights went out in the house. My mother cut the electricity and rushed to hide my brother and me. She thrust us between the heavy curtains that divided the living room and dining room just as my father came in the front door.

"Laurent," was the only thing she said before he hit her. Fils and I held each other as we listened to my father beat my mother, the blows landing again and again. I wanted to run from our hiding place and do something, anything, to help her, but what? I'd be overpowered, and then there would be no one to protect Fils.

My mother moaned as my father dragged her down the hall to the bedroom. She gave herself to him, and I knew it was to save us. This happened over and over again in our new home. Our lives in that house became a living hell.

In our culture, what my father was doing to our family was shameful, and that's why we had to keep it secret. His actions would have been considered craziness, and in our society if you were a child of a crazy person, you were considered crazy too. No matter how battered we were in the mornings, we were never allowed to tell anybody what was going on inside our home. "It's for our own good," my mother told us. My father was a highly ranked soldier. In the eyes of our neighbors we were rich. We were the lucky ones.

My mother's pregnancy was growing by the day, but it didn't change my father's violent behavior. I dreaded the night. Each day I woke with fear, and the sick knowledge that all too soon it would be nighttime again. My mom became a hardened woman. She became so tough that Fils and I were scared of making any mistakes around her. The slightest thing could set off her anger.

After one particularly bad night, my mother had to be taken to the hospital. I left school to go see her and was shocked to find her unconscious in a hospital bed, her face swollen and bloodied. A thin sheet stretched over her belly, which rose and fell in rhythm with her breathing. She was smaller than she had been when she entered the hospital. She'd delivered the baby boy. The doctors told me they didn't think she would make it. Everything in the room was so quiet, I became scared.

I prayed to God, *Please let my mother get well. Please help me. Please let her get well.* Eventually, she awoke.

"Mama, I'm here," I said, sending up a silent prayer of thanks. She looked at me and tears started flowing down her face. I hugged her and couldn't help but cry too.

Haltingly, she whispered in my ear, "Dydine, I want you to look after your brothers. Never depend on anyone. From now on, you don't have a mother or a father. I'm so sorry for everything. I never wanted your life to be like this..." She sank back into the pillows and closed her eyes.

I looked up, trying to hold back my tears. *I'm only seven years old*, I thought, *how will I take care of my siblings?* My tears spilled over and I cried as hard as I ever had before. Harder even than when I was with Auntie Agnes during the killings and the bombs that were exploding around us. I don't know when the doctors came in, but they grabbed me and took me away. Vestine, our babysitter, arrived to take me home. As we walked back to the house, I felt like a robot. I couldn't hear the cars, bikes or any sounds at all. My world was ending.

I tried to shake it off and be brave as my mother had taught me to be. I needed to learn how to take care of Fils, and my new baby brother Boris, and how to cook for them. I had to keep the pride of our family, as my mother always said. *Never let anybody know your problems*, I heard her voice in my mind. *People like to hear good things, not bad ones. Always smile, look clean, never tell anybody that you are hungry, nobody wants to hear that.*

One morning days after I visited my mother, a car came down the road and parked in front of our house. My mother stepped gingerly from the car, my beautiful new baby brother Boris in her arms. I screamed loudly, calling for Fils. We shrieked and whooped and rushed out the door to help my mother inside.

After my mother's return, I was hopeful things would change. Boris was a happy baby, and there was so much excitement over him in the house. For a few brief weeks, Fils and I slept through the night again, waking only to Boris's tiny muffled cries when he woke for his nighttime feedings. Then, without warning, the beatings began again.

One morning after one of my father's bad nights, my mother told my father she was leaving him and taking us with her. She had us dressed and packed, and hurried us toward the front door. "You can't be around the kids anymore, Laurent!" she said.

My father grabbed her arm. "Please don't leave me alone," he said. "Forgive me, Devota! Please don't take my children away from me." A ragged sob tore from my fathers' throat, as he slumped into a chair at the kitchen table and held his head in his hands.

My mother held the doorknob in her hand, then slowly released it as my father's sobs filled the room.

"I am begging you, I am begging you," my father repeated.

Mom ushered us back into the hallway to our room, gently pushed us inside and closed the door. Fils and I pressed our ears against the wood to listen. The sound of my dad's crying filled me with hopelessness. My life was nothing but pain. I wished I could bring back father's whole family so peace could finally return to our home. I wished he could be whole again.

"Devota, stay a little longer, come and sit down with me," he pleaded, "and help me cry for all our people that were killed horribly for nothing. Please help me cry because my own tears will never be enough for my family."

We stayed. I knew that all my mother had ever wanted was to have a normal family. I knew this because it's all I had ever wanted as well. It's difficult to give up on a dream.

It was true that Laurent sometimes showed encouraging signs. The months of March through July, the months of the Genocide, were the worst; those months were hell for my family. But other months Laurent could be a wonderful father. He'd arrive home with a bottle of champagne for my mother and pick us up and toss us high in the air until we couldn't stop laughing. He would sit at the table with us and help us with our homework and even take us to school sometimes. Giving up on Laurent meant giving up the good times as well as the bad, and my mother wasn't ready to let the good in him go.

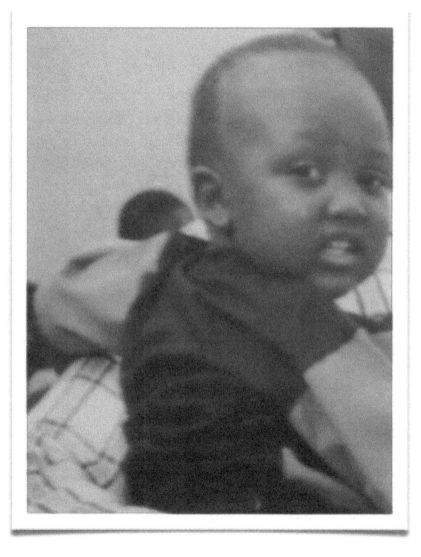

Baby Boris

Chapter Eleven: Nightmares

Our lives improved for a time. After Dad's breakdown at the kitchen table, he tried so hard to focus on us and not on his past. When he slept soundly, my nightmares seemed to take over as my tormenter. Mom didn't understand what was happening to me, why I couldn't sleep through the night without waking up screaming. She asked me repeatedly to tell her of my dreams, but I couldn't find the words I couldn't put together pieces of flashback of my life during the Genocide.

Finally, when I was eight years old, she managed to get me to reveal the location of my terrible dreams. They were always in Rwamagana. I never would have told her if I knew she would try to take me back there. I suppose she thought it would be healing, that perhaps by revisiting the places that tormented me in my dreams, I might see there was now nothing to fear.

We rode a bus together back to Rwamagana, and walked the still-familiar road to my grandparents' house. My palm was sweaty in my mother's hand, and my heart seemed to be thumping so loudly in my chest, I wondered whether she could hear it. We approached the neighbor's house, where I had stood in line with the other Tutsis on that first morning of the killings. Memories flooded back in pieces. I saw the flash of machetes rising and falling, and heard the screams and grunts of the others as they were cut down, one by one.

I began to shake and cry and my feet refused to move. My mother tugged gently on my hand to pull me forward and seemed surprised when I wouldn't budge. She squatted down in front of me so our faces were level and coaxed me with soft words of encouragement that grew firmer and more forceful when she realized they weren't working.

I remembered everything. The animal, metallic stench of blood mixed with dirt. The frantic, high voices of grown adults who pleaded for their lives. The shrill whistles the Hutus blew as they celebrated their kills. I was overwhelmed with the worst feeling I've ever experienced, and I thought I might pass out right there on the road. My mother should never have brought me here. I closed my eyes tightly and with all the strength I could muster I willed my body to disappear, to transport me to any place else.

"Dydine, what's happening to you?" Mom asked, panic rising in her voice. "Everything is OK. Tell me what you're feeling."

Don't go there! I wanted to scream. *Everyone who goes there dies!* But I was mute. Finally, my mother scooped me up in her arms and continued walking with me down the road. I was too big to be carried in such a way, but any embarrassment I might have felt was overwhelmed by fear. I buried my head against her chest and tried to calm my stomach. A sour taste had crept into my mouth, and I worried I would be sick.

Outside this Hutu neighbor's house, an old woman sat in the sun. Mom set me down and I clung to her leg, still shaking. "I'm your neighbor, a daughter of Yohana Baptist," my mother said to the woman. "May I speak to you?" she asked.

The woman just looked at us, saying nothing.

Mom gestured at the house. "Is anybody there?"

"I'm here. This is my home," the old woman said.

My mother began making introductions, but before she could say my name, the old woman jumped up and reached out for me. I flinched and drew back behind my mother's skirts.

The woman's eyes were soft and wet. "My God," she whispered. "I wish my husband was still alive. Nothing would make him happier than to know this little girl survived. He saved her from the others."

"What do you mean?" my mother asked.

The old woman went into the house and returned with a sweet snack. I wasn't hungry, but I thought eating something might settle my stomach so I accepted. It seemed to give the woman great pleasure to feed me. I didn't remember her, but clearly she remembered me. My mother told me to play while she spoke with the woman. The raw terror I felt at being back in this place had subsided somewhat by then, but I remained jittery and nervous. I drew a stick in circles through the dirt, trying to busy myself, trying to forget the scene that had played out years ago during the genocide when I stood here clutching my jar of milk, while the terrible giants loomed over me, making fun of me and waiting to kill me.

Those years ago, as my life hung in the balance, it was the elderly Hutu man, Mujyambere, the old woman's husband, who got to me first and put me between his legs.

"I swear, I'll kill the next one of you that tries to touch this child," he told the other men. "You'll have to kill me first before you kill her."

I remember the confusion on the faces of the killers. They could have easily overpowered him, but it would have been dishonorable to murder an elder especially when it was your own father. Eventually, they lost interest and went in search of other victims, and the old man took me inside his home and pushed me under an old wooden bed.

Now noises emerged from the house; the sound of my mother crying, of the old woman trying to comfort her. I could see them through the open door, and they both kept looking at me as though they were talking about me. Then they stood up and began to walk around the home, as if the old woman was showing my mother something, as if they were on a tour.

My mother returned and hugged me so tight I could feel her heart racing. I let her hold me and told her she would be fine, using the same tone and soothing words she used for me when I needed comfort. This brought a smile to her sad face and she wiped the tears from her eyes and said, "Let's go, Sweetheart!"

The old woman followed us with her eyes as we left the yard. I sensed that she must have told my mother something bad. As we walked, my mom's mind seemed far from where we were. She looked at me like she didn't know me. We walked toward my grandparents' banana plantation and sat there for a while. A warm breeze lifted and stirred the leaves on the trees.

"Dydine," my mother began. "I'm so sorry that I had to leave you behind." She gently cupped my chin in her hand and raised my face to look at hers. I didn't want to meet her gaze but I did.

"Please know," she said, "I had no other choice. I'm so sorry I wasn't there for you when you needed me most. I'm here now, and nothing will ever separate us again."

She cried as she spoke, and I felt suddenly embarrassed to have caused her pain. I wanted her tears and the pain to end.

"Mom, will you tell me one of your stories?" I asked.

She wiped her face and began to tell me my favorite story of Keza. I leaned into her arms and began to fall asleep, listening to her beautiful voice.

When I woke up, we were in a taxi arriving back home in Kigali. No sooner had we arrived to the house than Fils rushed to me and my mom, telling us dad had been acting crazy while we were away. He was confusing names again, calling Fils by his brother Safari's name. He'd been drinking all day and screaming at the Hutu neighbors.

"He scares me," Fils said.

My mother held us both tightly against her and looked up to the ceiling, her lips murmuring a silent prayer. I knew she was asking God to protect us, to heal my father once and for all. I followed her eyes with my own. *Yes, God,* I thought. *What else must we survive?*

When I was nine, my mother had another baby, a girl named Bettina, and I thought having a little sister was the best thing that had ever happened to me. I couldn't wait to share a bed with her, tell her my secrets and talk about girl stuff. I was so excited to learn how to change her diapers and help my mom feed her.

Bettina was born on April 2nd, approximately the same date as the start of the Genocide. My father was so sad that his family couldn't be with him to share the happy news of his daughter's birth. His grief triggered something within him. That night he became violent, but my mother was still so weak from having the baby that he turned his attentions to us. I grabbed little Boris, and Fils and I ran outside into the night.

The year of Bettina's birth was the year that most survivors were trying to find the bodies of their loved ones and give them a proper, respectful burial. Of course, my father couldn't find his brother's bodies. They had been thrown into the unknown pit. My father's rage lasted well into the next day. He crushed everything in our house, the radios, the TV, the chairs... He buried them in our back yard and sat on top of the mound, drinking all day. By nightfall, his eyes were so red that you couldn't recognize him.

My mother's family came to the house and begged her to leave him. By this time, however, my mother had made up her mind. She wouldn't leave Laurent, she told them, because we were the only family he had left. It would kill him, she said.

It almost killed you, I thought, but even as I rued her choice, I understood her confusion. She never gave up hope that my father would get over what had happened and move forward with her to help raise their children.

Mother may not have given up hope in my father, but her family gave up hope in her. Frustrated that she wouldn't change her situation, they refused to talk to her. Rumors about our family were spreading. We were making the rest of the family look bad. Still, my Mother had always gone her own way, and she would not be swayed. We would be beaten in the night and put on a smile the next morning and go to school.

Once I heard some of my fellow students saying bad things about my dad and how crazy he was. When I came home and told my mother, she switched us to a new school.

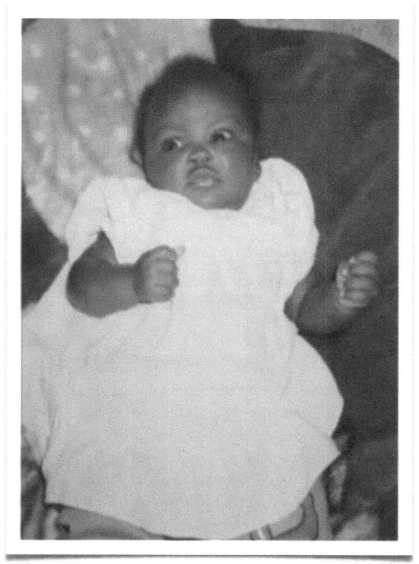

My Little Baby Sister Bettina

Chapter Twelve: The Cold Wedding

As conflicted as my feelings about my father might have been, I desperately wanted my parents to get married. Because they had never had a proper wedding, the other children in the village sometimes called me and Fils bastards. I would go home crying, asking my mother over and over again when she and my father would get married. Her answer was always the same: *Once your dad gets well, then we'll have a wedding. And you'll be even luckier than all your friends, because you'll get to attend your parents' wedding party!* My mother and I would have fun talking about it, imagining what she'd wear and how she'd do her hair. Like most other young girls, I loved to daydream.

My father never did recover, but the day arrived when my parents did get married. Maybe my hounding questions finally wore my mother down. Maybe she decided to have the wedding to preserve the thing she valued above all else: our family's good name. Maybe she did it out of respect for Laurent's mother, to fulfill my grandmother's prophecy that we would be the only blood from her family to survive. Whatever the reason, I know she did not do it for herself. She must have known on some level that marrying my father was tantamount to suicide.

I believe she did it for us. She made a sacrifice for her children so they could live without stigma. Her family thought she was insane. *Devota, have you lost your mind?* My Uncles asked. They begged her to reconsider, told her she was still young enough to meet someone else, but she refused. My mother always made her own decisions. She was not one to be easily swayed by the opinions of others. When her family insisted on canceling the wedding, my mother refused, and so they told her not to come running back to them when times got difficult. She was on her own now.

At the age of 28, my mom married my dad, still hoping she could somehow bring him back to life. When the big day arrived, I was so excited to wear my new fancy clothes. We kids had never experienced a celebration like this, and I was elated that for once people were gathering at our house for something good. We'd never had a birthday party, or Christmas or New Year's parties. All those days had been nightmares for our family. They somehow provoked my father's fear the Interahamwe were after us, and stoked his desire to hunt and kill us himself, to save us from a Hutu massacre.

My parents' wedding had become an almost mythic event to Fils and me. It was the realization of our long held dream to be a normal family, and we couldn't believe we were actually getting our wish. At night, we whispered between our beds about the details we'd overheard the adults planning. We discussed in detail what we would wear, what food we would eat, whether there would be flowers and dancing. We wondered aloud whether the wedding might cure our father. We thought the wedding was capable of changing everything.

That day, we kids whooped and hollered and ran around drinking soda that our family normally couldn't afford. We met new kids, played and laughed and stuffed ourselves with sweets.

Dydine Umunyana

It was a beautiful sunny day, and one of the happiest times I could remember. My mother's family attended the ceremony but was stoic by comparison; they couldn't fake happiness for what they viewed as such a disastrous event.

My mother looked beautiful, but I sensed a sadness inside her and as the day wore on I grew increasingly worried. It was supposed to be the most wonderful day of her life, the day Devota had dreamed of for years and years since she had met Laurent for the very first time. But neither she nor my father smiled during the ceremony. My father seemed like he was in a hurry, like he was waiting for the guests to leave. My mother hovered nervously, afraid he would lose it in front of all the guests. In the photos, she looks terrified.

As night approached and the party wound down, my fears intensified. I'd never had a day like this before. I wanted so badly for everything to go well, but night was coming and I prepared myself to run and hide again. I felt so incredibly tired. I craved a long night's sleep, but it was not to be. That same night of the wedding, my dad began cursing the Hutus, first quietly, then screaming so loudly I was certain all our neighbors could hear him. In that moment, I hated the Hutus as well. They had ruined this day for me. They'd ruined everything. Even our great celebration could not break the Genocide's hold on my father's fragile mind.

I finally understood; I didn't have a family, we'd never be a family, and I really was alone. There was no need to live if things would never change; my life was exactly what the Interahamwe always wanted for us: worse than death. I couldn't imagine how such a beautiful moment in our lives could be so thoroughly ruined.

My father became hysterical, sobbing and then yelling and threatening to hunt us to death. We now knew what to do in these dark moments, how to hide and escape. First, my mom turned off the electricity so my father would think the power was out in the whole neighborhood. We'd hear his voice in the darkness, coaxing us to come out, saying he just wanted to kill us nicely to save us from a worse fate. Then his tone would grow meaner and he'd scream for us to come out and die like soldiers, instead of waiting for the enemies to find us and kill us. My mother would put Bettina on her back, and our babysitter Vestine would carry two-year old Boris. Mom would grab Fils's arm while I ran after them outside the house. Then my mother would lock my father in the house before he could chase and shoot us.

That's how we always did it, but one night something went wrong. In the darkness and confusion, my mom locked me in the house with my father. I'd been by her side, almost out the door, when I remembered how cold it was and had run back to my room to grab a sweater. Thinking I'd already made it out, she'd locked the door. It was so dark, Mom never saw me waving to her from the window, begging for her to wait for me. I was locked in the house with a mad man, and my mind flew in a thousand directions. I struggled to calm myself, to think. I was running out of time and I had to act quickly to save myself.

My dad was wearing white shorts, which made it easy for me to see him in the dark. As he crashed through the house, smashing whatever was in his way, I quietly dodged him, moving among the different rooms. My mother must have realized I wasn't with them. I was searching for a new place to hide when I heard her voice whispering my name through the open window in our room. I ran toward her voice, almost crying with relief. I was about to climb through the window to join them when my father entered my room. He must have heard my mother's voice as well.

Mom screamed when she saw him behind me. I heard his footsteps bearing down on me and quickly slid back and ducked around him into the hall. Dad couldn't see me, but he knew I was in the house. He chased me back and forth from room to room, screaming my name. I ran until I couldn't run anymore, and then I remembered that somewhere in the closet was a big metallic box where my mother stored extra blankets and sheets. Fils and I always played hide and seek in the box, and I thought I could probably still fit inside it and wait for my father's rage to pass. I jumped in and closed the lid. After a moment, I heard footsteps enter the room, accompanied by my father's heavy breathing.

"I know you're in here!" he screamed. He tore the room apart, his frustration growing, and then he took his gun and began shooting blindly. I waited to be shot. I lay back against the blankets and pulled another one over my head. A steely calm came over me. I was so comfortable inside the box, where it was warm and soft. We live and then we die, I thought. I waited for my death.

Someone knocked at the front door and Dad left the room to see who was there. I scrambled out of the box and slipped out the window. My mother and siblings were waiting outside for me, and they cried with relief when they saw me. They seemed more scared than I was. They'd been waiting outside for hours and it was very cold. We walked for miles trying to find a place to hide where we couldn't hear my father's screams. We went to the Catholic Church, thinking the church would be open but the doors were closed. Eventually, we settled in the doorframe of a small house beside the church, cuddling close for warmth while my mom told us stories. At some point, I fell asleep.

The next morning, we crept back to the house. Everything was quiet, but the house was in ruins. Dad was always exhausted after these long nights, and he would usually sleep for a day, sometimes two afterwards. When he woke up, he wouldn't remember anything at all. *What happened?* He'd ask. *What happened?*

We showered and began putting on our school uniforms, as we did every morning.

"No!" my mom stopped me, as I was zipping up my uniform. "You're not going to school today. We're going someplace else far, far away. Our life is going to change for the better, starting right now."

She packed several bags and called a taxi to take us to the bus station. "Help me pack, Dydine," she said, tossing blankets at me. "We're going to flee, far away from your father. I won't do this anymore. We're going to Uganda."

I was giddy hearing her words, maybe from exhaustion and lack of sleep. I laughed. I couldn't help myself. "Mom," I said, "we didn't even get to Uganda when we were fleeing the Interahamwe, and now we're going all the way to Uganda just to flee from dad? Why did you even marry him?"

Her slap was swift and forceful, and my hand flew to my stinging cheek before I had time to realize what had happened. Mom's face was furious. I'd never seen her so angry.

"Shut up, you stupid girl!" she screamed. "I did it for you. All my horrible life is a sacrifice I made for you."

I was too stunned to speak. We rode in silence in the taxi. I wanted to cry, but I was too scared to utter a sound. I must have done something wrong, I thought. I must have been cruel. I'd meant it as a joke, to try to release the tension from the situation, but instead I'd struck a nerve. *She hates me.*

Eventually, Mom calmed down. She turned to me. "Your father will meet us where we're going. It's just not possible for him to come with us at this time."

As she spoke the words aloud, a shriek of protest rose to my lips, but the sound never came out. In an instant, I realized what I truly wanted now: to be away from my father. The events of one day and one night had shattered my naïve belief our family could be made whole again. I knew that was impossible now. I was forging a new notion of family: one without my dad. Why couldn't my mother see it too?

When we boarded the bus, Mom told us she didn't want any jokes from us, she didn't even want to hear our voices. We took a seat in the middle of the bus, mom at the window with Bettina, Fils in the middle, and me on the aisle with Boris on my lap. I snuck a look at my mother. Her mouth was set in a grim, determined line. She didn't look like my beautiful mom anymore. She was an angry woman, a stranger. Mom turned her body away to face the window, and as her shoulders began to shake, I realized she was crying. Her tears triggered my own, and suddenly we were all crying on the bus. Mom reached around Fils to me and pulled us all in for a tight hug.

"We're OK," she said. "Everything is going to be all right." But the look on her face was so sad and weak that I knew she was pretending.

Nine hours later, we arrived in Kampala, Uganda. We'd all fallen asleep and another passenger shook us to wake us up. Kampala bustled. People swarmed the streets, everyone selling or doing something. People were eating outside, selling fruits, speaking quickly in Luganda and Swahili. No one spoke our native language Kinyarwanda, and we didn't know Luganda. In the little Swahili she knew, Mom asked for directions to a cheap motel. She paid for one room for all five of us, and once we got inside, we collapsed on the bed and slept until the following day when the housekeepers arrived to clean the room.

Back in the motel lobby, Mom asked the workers about rental houses, and some of the girls who worked there took us to a place where we could rent a house for a few months. It wasn't much, but it bought us time for mom to figure out our next move.

I on the right / Fils in the plain white shirt / Boris the smallest and cutest person in front.

Chapter Thirteen: Life in Uganda

My mother seemed ready to embrace our new life. As we moved into our rental home and began putting our things away, She called us into the living room and sat us all down.

"Listen to me, all of you! There are new rules in Uganda. You must stay in the house at all times. There are people here who steal kids. We have to stay together, and I need your help. This is a new country and we'll only be here a short period of time. There's a good chance we'll be moving to Europe so your father can get the help he needs. Then we can be a family again."

My mother had been talking to her friend Paul. Paul was from Belgium and was married to a Rwandan woman who was a good friend of my mother's. He was the one who gave her the idea to go to Europe. Paul was one of the few people who seemed to understand my father's condition. He urged my mother to take my father out of Rwanda to seek special treatment abroad. He sounded so confident when he told her that then our father would be well again.

My mom convinced my father to come meet us and leave everything in Rwanda behind. As a soldier, however, it was impossible to leave the country without permission, so he remained in Rwanda while we waited for him to be granted leave. In the meantime, I was looking forward to several good nights of sleep. Our new home had one bedroom, a living room and a kitchen. Mom and Bettina slept in the bedroom and the rest of us slept in the living room on the new mattress mom bought. In the living room, there was a small square window through the wall, and when the sun rose and hit it, it would flash light through the room and wake me up. I loved following the beam of light across the floor.

To pass the time, my mother told us stories of triumph from the bible, the story of Abraham and his family, and Joseph, and the story of Job. Those were our favorites. My mom memorized them and made up songs she inserted into the stories so we wouldn't get bored. When she reached a sad part in a story, she would cry and we'd go to her and hug her tightly in our arms. We would smile at each other with smiles that were both happy and sad at the same time. Together, we watched the sun rise.

"Someday," she said, "we'll laugh about this. You know? There is a beautiful life waiting out there just for us! We just need to hold on and work together to get through this."

We were in the new house for almost three months when my mother was summoned by the Rwandan military to return to Kigali. Her husband was in jail, they told her, and they wanted her to sort out his problems. He was a valuable soldier, they said. One of their smartest men, and they needed him in good shape.

That night I woke to the sound of someone crying. I rubbed the sleep from my eyes and went to investigate. I found my mother crying in her room.

"Mama, what happened?" I asked in a soft voice, so my brothers and sister wouldn't wake up.

She pressed her palms to her eyes and rubbed the tears from her cheeks.

"Forget everything I said before, Dydine. Life has to be hard." Her voice was choked with sadness and anger. It was almost unrecognizable from the beautiful voice that comforted us and read us stories.

The next morning she gave us food, drinks and books. "Dydine, no one is to leave the house," she said. "I'll be gone just for a few days." She turned to Boris and Fils. "You boys listen to your sister. Don't disobey her, Don't leave the house. Play inside. OK!"

With a final reminder to me to care for my brothers, mom gathered up Bettina, who was just one and still a baby, and left the house to return to Rwanda. I was only nine years old and couldn't believe she'd left us alone, in a strange country, where they spoke a different language. I was terrified.

For three long days, we waited indoors for our mother to return. On the first day, our independence seemed like a luxury. We played all day long and could sleep as much as we wanted. We could sleep all night in peace! But then we grew bored, and by the second and third days, the house became like a jail to us. We sat, looking through the window, hoping to see our mother returning home. I imagined her bright face, the ever-present red lipstick she wore when she went out. Even after the long bus ride, I knew she'd return looking clean and fresh. We waited and waited, and then we waited some more.

On the third day, a strange man walked close to our window. He wore formal clothes, a white shirt and black slacks, and he snapped his fingers as he whistled a song. We were so starved for interaction with the outside world, Fils and I leaned out the window and said hello to the man. Hello was one of the only words we knew in Luganda, but he answered us in our maternal language, Kinyarwanda. He looked up to the window and broke into an easy grin. His face was young, maybe thirty years old. We talked through the window for such a long time, Fils and me asking him questions so he wouldn't leave. It had been so long since we'd met a person who knew our language and he was so friendly to us that we didn't think of him as a stranger anymore.

We begged him to come into the house and play with us, and he accepted. We opened the door for him, and he sat with us and chattered away until we began to feel as though we were talking to someone in our own family.

"Do you know a Rwandan that owns a store around this neighborhood?" the man asked.

"Yes, we know him and it's not far from here," I responded.

"Can one of you come with me and show me where the shop is? I have a car, I will drop you back here in few minutes."

Fils and I exchanged glances. He tilted his head and lifted his eyebrows twice. It was such a silly face, I broke out laughing.

"Dydine, please let me go," he whined. "I know where the store is."

"No, don't even think about it, mom told us not to leave the house." I said.

"Come on, kids, it's just a few minutes," the man said. He turned to me. "Let me take your brother and I'll soon bring him back to you."

I hesitated then gave in. "Ok, Fils, go with him but make sure you come back soon. Mom is coming back today, and you have to be here before she gets home, OK?"

Fils left happily with the man. He was so excited to be outside of the house, and to get to ride in a nice car. This was his lucky day!

While Boris and I waited for Fils, we wondered aloud whether Fils and the strange man would bring us back candies. Boris wanted a chocolate bar, but I wanted a lollypop. You could make them last longer. When twenty minutes passed and there was no sign of Fils, we began to worry.

"Do you think I'm stupid?" I asked Boris. He was only three years old, and I was nearly ten, but he was the only person I had to talk to. Sometimes I spoke to Boris when I was really talking to myself. "I mean, letting Fils go with someone we don't know? You don't think the man would hurt our brother, do you? Mom said they eat kids in this country!"

Several minutes turned to several hours, and still we waited. We sat glued to the window, thinking any minute Fils would come bounding up to the front door. It grew dark outside, and I started to panic. Mom would be home any moment. They were only supposed to be gone for five minutes. I became terrified with worry and began to cry.

"Mom is going to kill me," I wailed to Boris. "She told me to look after you guys, and we don't even know the name of the man who took Fils."

A dog began to bark, and we rushed to the window thinking Fils had returned, but it was my mother. I could tell by the way she walked that she was in a bad mood. I was a dead person. How could I tell my mom what had happened? That her son had been missing since this morning?

Mom's expression was grim as she opened the door, and I thought perhaps someone had already told her about Fils. I jumped from my watch by the window and rushed to her. "Mom, you already know? Who told you?" Do you know where he is?"

"Who?" Mom asked, taking a sleepy Bettina from her hip and setting her gently on the floor.

"Fils!" Boris said.

"What, he's not here?" Mom asked. Then she started laughing. She pinched Boris's cheek. "Nice try, kids. It takes more than that to trick your mother. Fils," she called into the living room, "come out wherever you are!"

I realized she thought we were joking and looked at the floor. Her laughter faded when she saw how scared we really were.

She dropped her bags. "No," she said, shaking her head. "Don't tell me he's not here. How can I return to Rwanda with only three children when I left with four?" She sat down on the floor right where she was standing and cradled her head in her hands, crying. I was so scared, I couldn't say a word. She wiped her tears and lifted her eyes to mine. Her expression was cold, venomous. I braced myself for the worst.

"Dydine, don't make me regret the decision I made a long time ago. I should have aborted you before you were born! Don't you think I have enough problems? You are the worst older sister ever. How dare you let you brother, my son, go with someone that you don't even know?" Tears washed down my face like a river. She was right. I was so stupid. How could I have let Fils leave? If anything happens to him, I thought, I'll never forgive myself.

Mom began cursing me so loud that Boris inched backwards until his back hit the far wall of the living room. Mom collected herself and left immediately for the Rwandan store to ask if they had seen Fils. They told her they hadn't seen him all day, nor had they seen the man I tried to describe.

Luckily, the storeowner could guess the identity of the man and told my mother his name. When they called his phone, the man answered.

"It's Devota, the mother of the child you have!" she said, her voice high-pitched and breathless.

"Where are you? I'm coming to see you," the man said. "I'm so sorry I took your son without your permission."

Mom struggled to keep her composure. "Just tell me if my son is fine. I'm at the store."

"I'm coming right now," the strange man said and hung up the phone. Twenty minutes passed before the man showed up, looking terrified of my mother. When she saw him, Mom ran quickly to him, demanding to know where Fils was.

"He didn't know the way to the store," the man stammered. "He couldn't find the right street, so we drove for hours. Finally, I decided to bring him back home, but I stopped by a shop to buy him some bread first..."

"Get to the point!" my mother yelled, and I thought the man might collapse right there onto the floor.

"When I went into the shop, I left your son in my car," he sputtered. "But when I returned, he was gone."

Mom's hand flew to her mouth. Her eyes were huge and frantic.

"I asked everyone in the street but no one seemed to have seen him... all day I was out looking for him, but I have no idea what happened. Madam, I promise I'm not gonna breathe before we find him."

My mom took me home and telephoned the different TV stations to give them Fils's photograph and description. Soon stations across Uganda began to broadcast news of a missing boy. She announced she was going out in search of my brother and I was to stay behind with Bettina and Boris. Before she left, she fixed me with a withering stare. "I want all three of you in this exact same spot when I bring your brother back."

A few hours later mom came back home alone. She was desperate and mad at me at the same time. She looked at me with such disappointment, and I wished I could disappear. Her look made me feel like I was a nightmare to her. We sat in the living room all night, waiting for any news. No one said anything. We were all numb and scared. In the very early morning, someone knocked at our door. Mom rushed to the door, hoping to see Fils, but instead it was another strange man. He was tall and big, in a black t-shirt and jeans. His hair was in dreadlocks.

"I have found your son," he said calmly. "But you have to pay me first before I bring him to you."

This type of bribe was not uncommon, but from the way the veins stood out on my mother's neck, I could tell she was struggling to keep her composure. The man was so smooth and confident; you'd think he'd done this sort of thing dozens of times. Mom made the deal and paid him the money and we were all relieved when the man left the house. Five minutes later, he was back with our brother.

My mom hugged Fils like never before. "Don't you ever dare leave me," Mom said to him.

Fils was ashamed. He broke into loud, hiccuping sobs. He seemed so lost and tired, like he had been walking all day. We waited for him to calm down and relax.

"Tell me everything that happened. Where were you all day?" Mom asked.

"I tried to find the store, but I couldn't, and the guy said he was going to bring me back home. He was angry with me because I'd wasted his time. On our way home, he stopped the car and left me inside it. I watched him go into a house. I had no idea when he was coming back. Outside, there were some guys on the street who came up to the car. I was scared, so I left the car and ran into the house to find the man.

I thought the men on the street would eat me or kill me, but when I looked for the guy inside the house he wasn't there. When I came back out to the car, the car was gone too. I kept looking for the man all day, but I couldn't find him." Fils was talking nonstop. We listened, rapt and horrified.

"As I walked, I came across an auto race. The person putting the race on saw me and took me up to a high hill, where

I could have the best view. One guy was standing on another guy's shoulders, and then he put me on his shoulders too. They kept me with them until someone saw the news on TV and brought me back to you."

Mom began making the sign of the cross. "Let's get together and pray because only God still lends this life to us. He brought Fils back to us tonight."

We tried to smile like we always did after saying a prayer, but Mom couldn't. She seemed so sad, and I realized there was something she wasn't telling us. She asked us all to sit down and started telling us a story from the bible, the story of Joseph and how he was unloved by his brothers and then they sold him as a slave to Arabs and how later he became the favorite of Herod, the king of Egypt. She loved this story and always cried when she told it to us, but tonight she couldn't even finish it. She stopped in the middle and said simply, "We have to go back to Rwanda. We have no other choice. Your dad needs us more than ever before. We leave in the morning".

My heart started racing. I knew what was back home in Rwanda, and I couldn't take it anymore. I had this terrible feeling that mom was about to give us up, perhaps to one of her friends or maybe she'd leave us with my grandmother. But looking at the pain that was in her face, I knew that she didn't need any more questions or stress.

"Go pack your things. We need to catch the early bus."

None of us said a word. We just went to our room and began collecting our belongings. Boris had no idea what was going on. He and Bettina were too young to understand. Fils started muttering to himself, and shoving his things into a bag. "You said we would never go back there," he said, and my mom overheard him from the living room. She flew into the room and scared us both.

"I say we leave tomorrow morning and I don't want to hear any more complaints! Now, pack your things, and go to bed!"

My mom seemed so lost, her mind so far away. We didn't know what was going on in her head. We just knew we had to obey her and hope for the best.

Fils and I couldn't sleep and stayed up whispering. We knew misery awaited us in Rwanda, and we didn't want the night to end. We counted down the hours, one by one, until mom pulled the blankets off our bodies. Soon we were back in line, waiting for the bus. We braced for another nine-hour drive on the terrible road. The bus stank. It was stuffed with people and their various belongings. When we arrived in Kigali, I realized my mom wasn't getting up. She seemed off somehow.

"Mama, are you feeling ok?" I asked.

"I'm fine. Just take care of your brothers and don't you worry about me. I'm just a bit dizzy, but I'm going to be fine." I knew she was lying. She sounded so weak. I realized she was sick. I wondered if it was actually possible to become sick with worry.

Fils watching TV

Chapter Fourteen: Back Home

There we were, back in Rwanda, getting off the bus again in Kigali. It was late afternoon, and the sun cast long shadows on the parking lot pavement. Mom called a taxi and we loaded our things in the trunk, then headed to Nyamirambo, one of the four districts of Kigali; this is where my father's distant relatives lived and where my father was staying. An elderly man, a distant uncle of my father's, greeted us and led us into a modest house, down a short hallway to my father's room.

Dad didn't bother to get out of bed. He greeted us like we were strangers, never asking how we were. Mom assessed the scene and whisked us from the room. She gave us baths and put us all into one bed.

"Hey there! Sleep well and rest." She had her cheery fake voice on.

"Tomorrow you are starting in a new school!"

She kissed us goodnight and turned off the light. And that was our family reunion.

The next morning she woke up Fils and me and took us to our sixth school in three years. Starting over at a new school was the last thing I wanted to do. I hated being the new girl all the time, always having to re-learn the social landscape and make new friends. I was usually far behind the other students in class. I knew I wasn't stupid, but constantly having to play catch up was demoralizing. I tried not to grow too attached to any one place or person, because I knew how the pattern would go. Just when I'd begin to hit my stride, make new friends and improve my marks, it would be time to move again.

Only a few weeks into our stay, Dad started up again with the nighttime beatings. We weren't even in our own house. Mom was mortified that Dad would come after us in the presence of other people. In his drunken rages, he had no shame. At least they were family and not strangers who might spread rumors. Still, our hosts were quickly tiring of us, and one weekend the old man who had initially greeted us called my mother outside the house. I watched them quarrel from the living room window. My mom threw up her hands and stomped back into the house.

"Hey, children, come with me! I need some air." She swung Bettina onto her hip and grabbed Fils's hand. I followed her, dragging Boris along with me. We walked from the back yard of the house all the way to the Nyamirambo Adventist Church. As we walked, mom cried, and we knew whatever was happening was very bad. When we reached the church, she plopped down in the grass. Ripping fistfuls of grass from the earth and chucking it into wind, she said, "We are going to Rwamagana. We have to leave today." She hugged us hard and we all cried, even the little ones who had no idea what she meant. Then we walked back to the house, packed our things and returned to the bus stop.

On the bus to Rwamagana, she didn't look well. She seemed weak, deflated, and her beautiful coffee skin looked pale and waxy. My shoe was sticking to something on the floor of the bus. When I looked down, I saw blood everywhere, pooling at my mother's feet.

"Mom! You're bleeding!" I cried, but she didn't respond. Her head tapped painfully against the window, and I didn't know if she was sleeping or worse. The woman next to us saw the blood and screamed for the bus to stop. Everyone got off the bus, including my siblings and me. There were 18 passengers in total, all standing outside, trying to see what was happening. My mother was pregnant again, and she was losing her baby. Someone reached out from the bus, grabbed me and pulled me back aboard. "She's asking for you," a woman said.

I pretended not to be afraid as I approached my mother. She had been propped up with her back against the window, her legs stretched out in front of her, reaching across the aisle. She beckoned me close and whispered in my ear. "Keep my kids together. I want all my children to grow up together. Never let anybody tear you apart..." She drew a shaky breath and closed her eyes. "Do you remember your Grandmother's house?" she asked.

"Yes," I said.

"Take the ticket and take your brothers and sister there and tell them I'm not doing well. Tell them I was taken to the hospital." She touched my cheek. "But don't you worry, darling. I'll be fine."

An ambulance arrived to take my mother away. Strangers offered to look out for us on the rest of our journey while she was in the hospital, and I was frightened and wary as we waited for the bus ride to begin again. A woman gave us some oranges to eat for the road. Bettina sat on Fils's lap and Boris sat on mine because he was heavier. I tried to be brave, as my mother would want me to be.

A half hour later, we arrived at my grandparents' house. I was so scared we were about to lose our mother that I momentarily forgot about the killings. I couldn't take my eyes away from the window. It had been a long time since I'd been here, but I still remembered my favorite Eucalyptus tree, where I used to sit and watch for my mother. When I saw the tree, I yelled for the bus driver to stop. My Grandmother heard us from inside the house and came out to see who the visitors were. When she saw us, she drew us all against her bosom in a big hug, then stood waiting for mom to exit the bus. The bus driver pulled the doors closed and pulled away. Grandma looked so confused.

"Where is your mother?" she asked. "My god! My daughter is a monster. How could she send her kids to travel alone?"

"She's at the hospital, Grandma." Tears sprang to my eyes the instant the words flew out. I began to tell Grandma what happened and before I could finish, she was on her way out the door to catch a mini bus to the hospital.

Fils, Boris, Bettina and I sat and waited outside my grandparents' house. We counted the cars, trucks and motorcycles that passed by on the road. All we wanted was for our mother to return. Late in the afternoon, my siblings fell asleep and I wandered off to sit on my favorite tree, where I had waited for my mother so many times before. There was nothing left to do but watch and wait and pray for her to come back to us.

Two days later, my grandmother returned with my mother, and the next day we buried our newborn baby sister. Mom named her Narah. Dad never made it to the burial of Narah his child. It was a very sad moment in my family, all of us crying, even Bettina who didn't know what was happening. My mom was still in so much pain.

My grandmother's compassion didn't last long. We had only been at the house for a few days when she asked us to leave. Grandma and Grandpa were already looking after several of my orphaned cousins, and Grandma couldn't understand why she should have to take care of even more children, especially ones who still had both their parents. Shocked, my mother knew we had no choice but to return to Kigali with all four of us in tow.

She rented a one-room apartment for us in a compound with many small houses. It was crowded, smelly, the kind of place where everybody knew what you ate, even if you didn't cook it. We'd never lived ostentatiously, but before now it had always seemed we had enough. Now, it felt as though we had nothing. Some days we kids would find a neighbor with a TV, and we'd watch it from outside the window of their house. When the neighbors saw us they'd hide the TV or close their curtains.

Then one day my father showed up at the apartment. No one knew how he'd found us. Miraculously, he came in peace. He apologized to my mother and asked her to return to live with him in Ruhengeri. Dad seemed to be doing well. He sounded contrite and promised us that he would never hurt us again. Mom accepted, still hoping her children could experience paternal love. At least that was what she told me. I knew we were about to be thrown out of the rental house anyway.

As we packed our things yet again, my mother gave me her same phony speech about how our lives were going to change for the better now, and we would finally be a family again. I'd heard it all before. I started muttering to myself, kicking the dirt and scuffing my shoes. "Yeah, right. Dad will never change."

Mom heard me and came charging in. "What did you just say?" she yelled. "I didn't raise you to be disrespectful to adults. He's your father, and nothing will ever change that."

I knew she was right, of course, but as far as I was concerned, we were all better off without him.

We arrived in Ruhengeri at midnight and our father was waiting for us. I could smell the beer on him the moment we walked through the door. No sooner had we stepped across the entryway, when he locked the door behind us. His eyes were red from drinking, and his voice was gravelly, raw. "Did you think you could take my children away from me?" he asked my mother, drawing back his hand and smacking her across the face. Mom's head snapped backwards and she nearly lost her balance. Bettina, who was still in her arms, began to wail.

The blow only seemed to fuel my father's rage. "You women think you're so smart. And you stupid little kids…" He wheeled on us, and we backed up against the dining table. "Did you choose your mother over me? I'll kill you all tonight."

We didn't know the house, so we didn't know where to hide. We had no choice but to accept whatever was coming for us. My mom fought him off to protect us, trying to divert his attention to her, but it was impossible; he was too strong. "Run away!" she screamed at us. "Get out!"

I spotted a window in the children's new room and ran for it as fast as I could. I pushed it open and shoved Fils out first, then handed him the little ones. I jumped through the window and finally my mom followed too. Our neighbors heard the fighting and came out to see what was happening. One family felt so sorry for us, they invited us into their home and offered us tea. We sat at their table, most of us bleeding, as the wife of the family tried to bandage our wounds. Her five children watched us silently. We sat at their table until morning.

As it turned out, the family that had taken us in owned the house we were renting, where my father still remained.

They let us stay an additional three months with them until the lease was up and then asked us to move on. My mother begged to stay longer but the owner decided we weren't "the right kind of people" to have in their rental house. My mother's pride was stung. Preserving the honor of the family name was so important to her, but it looked like she was losing control even of that. We began looking for a new place to live.

We found a new home not too far away, in the same neighborhood. We could still attend the same school. Back together with my father again, we settled into our familiar pattern of living amicably during the day and fleeing in terror at night. We knew that no matter what happened inside our house, we had to keep it to ourselves, to wake up and put on a smile and go to school like nothing had happened.

One day, while studying in my class like a normal kid with a normal life, pretending I knew what that was like, I was pulled aside by the principal and told to go to the hospital. I froze with fear; the last time my mother went to the hospital, she had lost her baby. My heart was telling me it was bad news, and without knowing why, I began to cry. I ran as fast as I could to the hospital, the whole time praying my mother was still alive.

This time my mother was six months pregnant. I feared the worst. The previous night had been very bad. We ran for what seemed like hours. When I arrived at the hospital I found my mother weak but happy. She'd delivered my baby brother Olivier prematurely. The baby was beautiful and so tiny. I was overjoyed to see his little face. He looked so peaceful with his eyes closed. My mother looked far worse by comparison. Dad had beaten her severely, and she had wounds on her face and hands. She'd lied to the doctors and told them she fell on the stairs in our house.

Olivier's name was meaningful to my mother. It was the name she'd given Fils but my father had changed Fils's name to Aristide, which means "a son that was born in the absence of his father." I thought Olivier was so old-fashioned.

"Mom," I said, "can't we call him something cool?"

"Go home and prepare the room for the baby," was all she said.

Chapter Fifteen: To the Memory of Olivier

I was eleven years old, and this was the happiest day I'd had in a long time. I hugged my mother and ran, singing, into the street. It was a forty-minute walk home, and I smiled the entire way. A new baby brother!

As I drew close to our house, I heard voices yelling from within. People milled about outside the house, drinking. It sounded like there was a party happening. I was so confused. No one had been there when we left for school this morning, but now a dozen or more people had gathered. Had they heard about the baby and come to celebrate his arrival? I had no idea what was going on, and I doubted my mother knew about this either.

When I opened the door, my mother ran past me, screaming. I had no idea how she got home from the hospital before I did; someone must have given her a ride. Mom screamed for my help and told me to run at the same time. I didn't see Olivier with her. I had the strongest sense that if I went inside the house, I would die.

Suddenly, my father was behind my mom with a gun in his hands. Mom ran into the kitchen with my dad right behind her, then she darted outside and locked the door. Dad banged on the door, screaming.

"You think I'm unable to raise them!" he said. "You should thank God that you ran into a Tutsi home. If you'd run into a Hutu home, I'd have burned you out! I would have burned the house and everything else inside it. Just like they did to my family!"

Dad went to his room where Olivier's body was, and I slowly crept into the kitchen and fled Outside. I heard dad firing his gun and I knew I must run again, this time far away from home. I turned on my heel and fled. I looked back only once, and when I did, I saw my father's face staring back at me from behind the window of the front door. The image of him at that moment haunts my memories.

Finally, because of the gunfire, the police came and intervened. I learned Olivier had died at the hospital. My father, who had been celebrating the birth with his drinking buddies, was already drunk by the time he'd learned of the baby's death. Dad struggled against the police as they took him away.

"I have to bury him as a hero! He's the child of a soldier!" he cried.

It was the custom in our culture for a soldier to fire his weapon in salute when he lost a son, and it was a terrible thing for a father to miss his son's burial. Still, the police had to bring him in. Gunshots could not be ignored.

Dad spat in the dirt. "you stupid policemen. You can't put me in jail. I'm a highly ranked soldier. You'll regret this, I promise!"

I watched him go, fighting with the police the whole way, but there were so many of them and they were stronger than he was. There was something satisfying about seeing my father physically restrained. I felt so relieved that he couldn't do any more damage, even though it pained me to see him so vulnerable.

One by one, my family members emerged from their hiding places in our neighbors' houses. Slowly, we gathered in front of the house. I had no idea where the people who were partying had gone. By the time we re-entered the house, no one was there. Mom sat us on the floor and held us, crying soundlessly. The next day, she organized the funeral of my baby brother. Olivier's death marked the second time my father could not attend his own child's funeral. My siblings and I all cried, but I noticed my mother was no longer crying. She looked different. Calm, angry, and sad all at once. I hoped she wouldn't become traumatized, like my father. I tugged at her sleeve.

"Ma, it's over. Let's go home. Take us home," I said.

She was so far away in her thoughts. She didn't answer, but let me steer her away. I was terrified of what would happen to us next. It seemed like a light had gone out inside my mother. I worried she had no more hope or love to give. Mom left the house without telling us where she was going. She returned two days later with no explanation, but I assumed she'd somehow once more negotiated the release of my father.

"Your dad is coming home tomorrow, and we're moving back to Kigali this week. Say your goodbyes to your friends."

My heart sank. I didn't think I could bear to be back under the same roof with my father. My mother must have seen it written on my face.

"Your dad isn't coming with us. He's going to finish his studies at Rwanda National University."

This was news! My father had always been smart, especially at math and science and I thought it would be good for him to be back in school, with assignments and research to occupy his time. I hoped it might distract him from his pain.

The next morning my dad arrived at the house looking scared and ashamed. He looked so slim. My mother had packed his things while he was away, and she hurried his goodbye. Even with my mom trying to move him along, my father dragged out the goodbyes. He seemed so sad, as though he was saying goodbye to us forever. Maybe he was, I thought, and felt hopeful, then chided myself for daring to want such a thing.

Our departure triggered a series of moves that proved devastating to my family's morale. We could never stay in any one place for long, either due to lack of money, or the chaos triggered from a surprise visit by my father. No one wanted us as neighbors. From house to house, city to city, school to school, we crisscrossed Rwanda. Everything in my life became temporary, and I no longer let myself become attached to people, places or belongings. I became a sad child. I didn't trust anyone.

My mothers's outlook darkened as well. She gave up trying to cheer and reassure us that everything would be OK. I used to loathe her optimism, but now I found I missed it. Perhaps she thought we were grown up enough to handle the truth, or perhaps she was just tired of pretending. Instead of nagging at us to smile and clean ourselves up so we looked presentable, she was constantly worrying about finances.

"How will I pay the rent, your school fees, and feed four stomachs with $100 per month. Do you think that's possible, kids?" she asked. "And I need a babysitter too. I have to work full time. You'll never see me anymore." She talked this way constantly, and we knew better than to answer her. We kept our heads down and attended to our chores. She was so testy, none of us wanted to draw her attention. I seemed to be her favorite target.

"Dydine, you have to help me raise your brothers and sister. I can't do it alone. I sacrificed so much to rescue you from your own father, so you'd better help me!"

I reeled at the unfairness of her words. *How is this my fault?* I wanted to scream, but I bit my tongue. I'd learned once Mom got going, it was best not to interrupt her, or I'd get slapped or worse.

"I wish I'd never had you in the first place," she would say wearily, her words landing like blows. "All my troubles started with you, Dydine. If I didn't have all you kids, I'd have a different life," she would say. "A happy one! But how can I remarry now? Who would love me?"

I let my mom's words roll around in my mind, and gradually, I started to believe them. It was clear that we kids were a burden. If mom wasn't so worried about providing for us, she could go back to being like she used to be, optimistic and happy. I began to believe something was wrong with me. Now, when the teachers at my new schools told me I was stupid, I believed them. Everything I did was wrong in one way or another. When Mom learned of my poor grades, she always said the same thing. "Your body grows, but not your brain."

After a recent growth spurt that also annoyed my mother (*More new clothes!*), I had become the tallest girl in my grade, something I loathed and was excruciatingly self-conscious of. In the past, when the schoolyard bullies of my classmates tore me down, I could at least go back to my mother for reassurance and support. Now, I got it from both sides. If I dared complain to my mother, she was insulted I should add to her worries.

"You don't realize what I'm going through, Dydine," she'd say. "Don't make me regret having you. I didn't want to give birth to you anyway."

More devastating than her words was their delivery. She uttered them without anger, just in simple, resigned sadness.

That's when I knew she was telling the truth. I was unwanted and unloved.

I began to wish my life would end. Life was so cruel, and I was so tired. I wondered why God would create life if it meant so much suffering. The only thing I could think to look forward to, was boarding school. In our country, it was customary for students to attend boarding school for high school, but not everyone went. You had to be smart and get good marks, and your parents had to be able to afford it or qualify for Surviver scholarship money. The odds seemed long in my case, but I began to wonder whether I might somehow be able to pull it off, if I worked very very hard. I had a few more years of primary school to figure out my plan.

One night I was in a very deep sleep, having a bad dream. An arm came through the window, trying to grab me and take me from my room. I heard a voice whispering my name and asking for help. Then the arm shook me, and I realized I wasn't dreaming at all. The arm was real! I screamed so loudly that Mom woke and ran into my room. She shrieked when she saw my father trying to squeeze through the bedroom window to get to me. She grabbed Fils and me and corralled all the kids into her room. We could tell Dad wasn't OK. No one knew how he had found us. We never told him when we changed our addresses.

Dad's voice called to me. "Dydine, my darling, open up for me, you know I love you so much. Don't be like your mother. It's so cold outside." His voice sounded so kind and loving. These were the first tender words I'd heard from an adult in so long. Something broke inside me and I started crying and trying to pull away from my mother to open the door for Dad. Mom wrenched me back to her so forcefully; I thought my arm would tear from its socket. Dad began gathering stones and throwing them through the windows. He smashed every window in the house. Terrified cries rose from the houses of our neighbors. No one knew this madman in the night. All they could see was that my family was attracting trouble.

We spent the rest of the night huddled in the hallway, where there were no windows, and miraculously, in the morning my father was gone. He would be back though, and so began a stretch of days in which our neighbors grew to hate us. Everyone had enough troubles of their own. No one needed more. No one wanted to be woken in the middle of the night by a mad man smashing windows. Dad came back again and again, always at night, always drunk, cursing my mother and screaming for his children. It didn't take long before the owner of our rental house told us it was time we moved on.

We moved a few more times, but each time my father found us. We never learned how. Eventually, Mother decided she had to bring us back to her parents' house. She knew they would open the door to her, even if only for a few days.

I liked being back together with my grandparents, in the familiar house, but I never kidded myself it was a permanent solution. Sure enough, one night I heard my grandparents arguing with my mother. They were worried my father would show up again, and they were too old to protect us, let alone themselves. There was also the matter of the additional crowding, and the extra mouths to feed. Grandma put her foot down and told my mother we had to leave. Grandpa looked away, saying nothing. He was always the sentimental one, but he wouldn't cross his wife in this decision.

That night, before she went to sleep, Mom came into my room and put her hand on my shoulder. "Dydine, I'm leaving. I'm going to Burundi, to look for a better future for all of you. Take care of your siblings." In the morning, she was gone.

I'd heard my mother talk about Burundi before. She thought we would be safe if she could find a way to move us all there. And once we were in Burundi, it would be easier for us to leave the continent! I don't know why she didn't take us with her. Maybe she couldn't afford to house us any longer, and she knew her parents would never turn us out. Whatever the reason, when she left for Burundi, I became like a mother to my three siblings. My childhood was abruptly over.

Life in Rwamagana wasn't always easy. Yes, we had the comfort of our extended family nearby, and it was wonderful to be reunited with Auntie Josephine and my cousins Kadafi and Mignone.... Auntie Agnes occasionally visited as well. She had married by then and was living in Kigali. We always looked forward to seeing her. In spite of the closeness of our family, we suffered. It seemed we were always sick with malaria, and we all struggled in school. I was so tired. I wanted to escape my life. I spent more and more time each day daydreaming of boarding school. I was convinced that once I was in boarding school, all my troubles would melt away. I could leave this life behind and pretend the past had never happened.

I couldn't help but miss my mother. No matter how angry I was with her, I prayed for her return. My siblings and I would sit in the front yard of my grandmother's house and imagine her coming down the road. We wanted to be the first ones to see her, so we could jump up and welcome her back.

We waited and waited, but mother never came. It had been well over a year since we'd had any news of her. Then one day, a friend of Grandma's raced up to the house. She told my grandparents that all Rwandans in Burundi were being killed! Tutsis and Hutus were attacking each other in Burundi. It was another civil war. She said that terrorists were burning buses, and that they'd probably burned the one my mother was on, and that was why we had not heard from her.

Grandma shushed the woman and hurried her out of the house, but we had already heard everything. It was the worst news I could imagine. I wandered away from my siblings toward a construction area in my grandparents' yard. I went inside an unfinished house and cried alone. I prayed to God. *If you truly exist, please bring back my mother.* I couldn't imagine living the rest of my life without her.

When I returned to the house, Grandma told me the woman who had visited us was a fool and didn't know what she was talking about. I wished her words could reassure me, but I trusted no one. I didn't expect any good act to come from another human being. The only thing I could think to do was write letters to God to express my feelings.

I had so many questions for him. I wanted to understand the nature of life, and why it was always so cruel. God was the only one I trusted to be truthful with me. I wrote and wrote, but of course God never answered. Soon my letters became stories, and sometimes my stories would become songs. Writing became a daily ritual, the only thing I looked forward to each day. I kept my soul alive by putting all my thoughts on paper.

When my mother did return to us, I was too weak to get up and greet her. I was recovering from another bout of malaria and still couldn't walk. I heard the excited trill of my siblings' voices and watched them jump up to hug a beautiful tall woman coming down the road. I couldn't believe my eyes. I wept with joy. Mother brought gifts for everyone. We were all so happy to see her. Even my grandmother, who was furious when she left, was overcome with relief. We all sat down at the dining table as Grandma bustled about the kitchen preparing an impromptu feast.

"I have good news, Mom," my mother said to Grandma. "Laurent has changed and he's been well now for almost a year." She leaned forward and gripped Grandma's hand across the table. "He wants the kids! He's finally ready to be a proper father to them."

Grandma drew back her hand. "Devota, we've heard all this before..."

Before she could finish, Mom interrupted her. "If the Interahamwe killers had not done what they did to his family, my children would have had a different life!"

Grandma was silent. Her eyes flickered to my face, and she could see I was stricken by the news. She looked away quickly and heaved a heavy sigh. I closed my eyes tight and beamed a silent message to Grandma. *Protect us! Don't send us back to him. Don't give us up, keep us safe!* I concentrated so hard on delivering the message, and the voice in my head was so loud, I felt certain it must work.

Grandma looked out the window. "Give him his children, Devota," she said wearily. "They are the only family he has left."

I was crushed. If I'd been standing, I'm certain my legs would have given out beneath me. I fixed Grandma with a nasty stare, but she wouldn't meet my eyes. She knew what would happen to us if we returned to Laurent. She just wanted us out of her house. Grandma was a shrewd woman. She had seized her opportunity to get rid of us.

Fils, Dad, Boris and me at our home in Kigali

Dydine Umunyana

Chapter Sixteen: We Are Christians

As with all our moves, it happened very quickly. One day we lived with our grandparents, the next we lived with our father. It had been over a year since we'd last seen him. I wasn't sure what to expect from this latest reunion, but it certainly was not the smiling, handsome straight-backed man who ran towards us to greet us.

Dad lifted Bettina from my mother's arms and tossed her in the air. She had no memory of our father, and giggled at the antics of this happy stranger. Dad approached me, Boris and Fils more cautiously. He crouched low so his eyes were level with Boris's, and he took Boris's hand in his.

"I'm so happy to see you all again," he said softly, looking each of us in the eye. "I promise from now on, things will be different."

I let him hug me. He even smelled different, clean like Nivea lotion. His eyes were clear with no hint of redness. Even so, I didn't believe him. I lay awake in bed that night, waiting for the screaming to begin. I was shocked when I awoke the next morning, having fallen asleep and slept through the night in peace. I didn't know what to make of it.

Our new life with our father was very structured. Dad worked all day, went to study every night, and attended church every Sunday. I'd never known life to be so organized, so predictable. I still waited each night for the old Laurent to return. I stared at the ceiling, running my escape route through my mind over and over, anticipating that first slam of the door, my mother's first scream. But they never came. Weeks passed, and slowly I began to relax. The old dream began to stir within me again, and I wondered whether my father really had changed, whether we could actually be the family I'd always wanted.

An unexpected addition to our new lives was the constant presence of prayer. We prayed first before eating and drinking, and we prayed before we left the house. We prayed for everything, and every other sentence from my father's lips was a quote from the bible. I didn't mind it. I loved this new, peaceful dad. He truly seemed to care about us and wanted to live after all. Now instead of dreading the nights, I grew fearful of the mornings. I worried one day I would wake up to find our new life was just a dream.

The church we belonged to was an enormous conservative Christian church. Nearly a thousand people attended each service. The new church had a lot of rules. No woman or girl could wear shorts or short skirts; we were only allowed to wear long dresses or long skirts. I didn't have anything that covered my legs, so the first time we went to a service together, Dad loaned me his long t-shirt. I was self-conscious in the giant shirt, which overwhelmed my small frame, but at least I was following the rules. There was also something nice about wearing my father's clothes. I felt I'd been claimed by him in some way that I hadn't been before.

And he seemed so proud as the pastor presented us to the congregation.

Just when the rhythms of our new domestic life became familiar, my mother shocked us by announcing she was leaving. She was going back to Burundi, she said, still working on her plan to get us out of the country, to start a fresh life somewhere far away. She promised it was temporary. She and my father argued, but I knew it was useless.

Once my mother latched onto an idea, there was no shaking her resolve. On the day of her departure, we accompanied her to the city of Butare, where she would take the bus to Burundi. We ate lunch at a restaurant named Credo. The meal was awkward for all of us. No one smiled or spoke. We concentrated on our food.

Suddenly my dad exclaimed, "We'll all be so much happier if you stayed!" Mom just looked at him as if she hadn't heard what he said. She'd finished her meal long before we had, and I could tell she was itching to leave. After the meal, she made me promise once more that I'd take care of my brothers and sister. I was furious with her for leaving us, but also scared and overwhelmed by how much I knew I'd miss her. I could barely meet her eyes.

She held me close. "Remember, Dydine, that everything in this world has an end. There is no rain that does not end and every ending is a new beginning! Just keep that in mind and wait for me. Just be strong as always," she said.

She walked a few steps away, then turned to look back at us. Tears streamed down her cheeks, and a loud sob tore from her throat. The sound of it shocked me. I watched her shoulders shake as she turned and walked away. I couldn't see her face, but I recognized her tears. They were the noisy, ugly kind, when you feel yourself unraveling. I wondered if she worried, as I did, that this would be the last time we'd ever see each other. I wondered whether without her here to protect us, my father would kill us. It was a great risk she was taking, putting her faith in my father's goodness, trusting he was better now. As always, she was strong in her convictions. She climbed aboard the bus and disappeared.

Without Mom around, Dad didn't seem to know what to do with us. We all looked at each other blankly, like we didn't know each other. I was twelve years old then, Fils ten, Boris five, and Bettina three. Bettina was the only one with the nerve to look my father in the eyes. The rest of us were too scared by what we might see. Slowly, we made our way back home.

The first Sunday without my mother, Dad woke us up earlier than usual in the morning to get us ready for church. I was relieved we were sticking to the routine.

"It's a big responsibility I have now," he said, sliding a clean shirt over Boris's head. "I have to thank God for the change in my life, and pray for the courage and ability to care for you properly."

Dydine Umunyana

The previous Sunday, the pastor of the church had asked my father if one of his children could address the congregation. He wanted us to tell our story, how God in his mercy had healed my father and set our family on a better path. I was shocked when Dad asked me to speak on behalf of my brothers and sister.

"Can I sing instead of speaking?" I asked. "I'm better off singing than speaking."

My father agreed. And so I was to perform in front of strangers for the first time.

When the time came, the pastor called Dad's name and asked him to bring his whole family up front. First, my father gave his testimony. Then the pastor gave me the microphone so that I could speak for all my siblings. I took a deep breath and started singing with my eyes closed.

I can recall every single word in the song. The words are written in my heart. It was a song that told our story in a way I knew I never could speak it. I poured my soul into my singing, wishing to express everything we'd lived through and everything we'd overcome. As I reached the mid point of the song, people in the church began to cry.

After church everybody came up to my father.

"What a blessed child you have!"

"She's got real talent!"

"God has given her a gift!"

I stood quietly beside my father, letting their words wash over me like a warm rain. Dad placed his hand on my shoulder, and looked down at me with pride shining from his eyes. I felt loved and safe. It was the happiest I had ever been in the presence of my father.

For a while he was the wonderful father I always hoped I might have. Every morning I woke up after a sound sleep, I truly did feel like a blessed child. We continued to go to church every Sunday, and I began to make new friends. Although I missed my mother, I felt as though we'd finally achieved the kind of normalcy I'd always craved. I allowed myself to start looking ahead again. I was in my last year of primary school. I was elated when Dad told me that after graduation, I would be headed to a boarding school just sixteen miles away.

Boarding school was my great dream. Once I was there, I could put my past behind me and start a new life. I'd sleep soundly every night, and never have to wake up listening for screams or slamming doors. I would never have to enter a room and search immediately for my escape route. Best of all, the friends I made in boarding school would be mine for years. In Rwanda, children attend high school for six years, first three years at one school, and then the last three years at another. Three years would be the longest I'd ever stayed in one place. Maybe I would make a best friend. Someone to confide in and whisper secrets to.

September arrived, and I packed my bags. As I folded my clothes in my suitcase, I imagined coming home for the holidays and telling my siblings stories about all the fun I was having with my new friends. I could feel my life changing; this was a whole new beginning. The only thing that marred my happiness was the nagging worry of what might happen to my siblings when I left.

My mother was still away and we didn't know when she might be back. Dad was doing so well, but I knew how quickly that could change. What would my brothers and sister do if they needed me and I wasn't there to defend them? I had promised my mother I would look after them. What if something bad happened while I was away? I pushed the thoughts back. *This is your chance, Dydine,* I told myself. *This is your chance at happiness.*

My new school was very beautiful, and I couldn't believe I would get to live there with girls and boys my own age. The buildings were all in the same style, set amidst lush gardens bursting with flowers. All the students looked clean and professional, the boys in dark blue pants with white shirts, and the girls in dark blue skirts with white blouses. The first night I slept in the dormitory, I smiled into my pillow. I was here. It was all real.

In many ways, boarding school was as I imagined, but some things took me by surprise. I began to realize how much independence I'd had living with my family. Although so much of my life often seemed beyond my control, I had often fulfilled the role of second mother to my siblings, and I was used to calling the shots on a day to day basis. At boarding school, everything was regimented. We all ate at the same time, went to sleep at the same time, and woke up at the same time. There was little room for individuality. It seemed like there were a thousand rules to learn and we were expected to obey them all.

The greatest surprise to me was how much I missed my siblings. I thought I'd be able to look ahead and not be pulled back into the drama of my past, but my thoughts turned to them constantly accompanied by my worries for their safety. I realized that I was wrong about being able to put my past behind me. My family, both the good and bad, was a part of me, and I would always carry it with me.

I wasn't the only one unable to forget the past. When I tried to make conversation with my new friends, I realized they had suffered much more than I had, they always reminded me of the lonely children I saw at the Army camp with my Cousin Kadafi after the Genocide. Most of them had lost their homes and gone to live in orphanages, where they were ignored, mistreated or worse. They didn't have parents or belongings to call their own. What they had seen during the Genocide was worse than what I had seen. Many of them had only one arm or were missing other limbs, which had been cut by machetes. Some of them witnessed their parents being slaughtered right before their eyes. One girl told me of watching her mother being raped. I realized how lucky I was.

When I had imagined my social life at boarding school, it was always a photographic image, a snapshot of me and my friends sitting together at a lunch table, laughing and chattering. Instead, my new friends only shared stories of pain. I sat silently and listened to them recount the horrors of their childhoods. I never participated in the conversation. I only listened. How could I share my misery, when I still had both my parents? My friends would say they wished they had a father like mine; they wished they had my life. The more I heard my friends talk about the dark times they endured, the more I felt like I didn't have a story to tell. I felt so lost.

Hearing the details of what the Hutu extremists did to my friends and their families stirred something dark inside me. The more I listened to their stories, the more my hatred for the Hutus grew. I began to feel uncomfortable sitting at the same table with children of the perpetrators. I started judging every new face I saw, trying to discern if they were Tutsis or Hutus. These stereotypes had been ingrained in me. I knew what facial features to look for that might distinguish a person. Silently, I sorted us all into our different categories.

I began to blame the Hutu children for what their parents did. I blamed these kids for every single horrible moment of my life and every misery my survivor friends had gone through. Hearing the others' stories re-awakened the nightmares of my own past. After a time, I found I couldn't even focus on my studies. My thoughts were of anger, hate, pain and revenge. When I sat alone to study, I'd start thinking about my life, my fears for my siblings, and at night, my terrible dreams returned.

Paranoia is a strange beast. When does it take hold of the mind? When do thoughts that might have seemed ridiculous or unbelievable at one time suddenly seem plausible? I began to fear that I was being watched by the Hutu students, and that I might be killed at any time. I no longer felt safe at school. I let prejudice poison my dream.

The more afraid I became, the more I pulled away from the other students. My mother's old words echoed in my mind. *No one wants to hear sad stories. You'll only drag them down.* Alone, I didn't have to worry about alienating anyone, and I could manage my pain. My one escape from suffering was through singing. I loved writing out all my feelings and making songs from them. Singing let me tap into the little bit of happiness left inside my heart. When I was singing, I could temporarily lose myself and forget my troubles.

I sought out places around campus where I could sing unnoticed. One day, while I was looking for a quiet place to sing, I heard other voices, beautiful voices united in chorus. I began to follow the sounds, and rounding a hallway I came upon the worship team choir. I tried to peek inside the open door of the practice room to glimpse the choir, and one of the students noticed me and invited me in. I was so shy, but listening to their voices, I immediately knew I wanted to be a part of the choir. I could feel it in my heart. This was where I belonged.

As I sat and listened to the choir finish their practice, thoughts whirled in my mind. *Was I good enough to join them? Who was I to even stand with them? Would they ever accept me?* When they finished singing, the choir huddled close together and began to pray. Many of them cried. It was so moving to watch. At the prayer's conclusion, everyone thanked God for the good things they'd experienced that week. It was their custom that everyone in the room had to speak and sing a little bit in turn. I was stunned when they invited me into the circle. Taking my cues from others in the group, I closed my eyes to listen to the different speakers. The oldest among us was eighteen years old; the youngest was twelve.

My heart raced as the girl beside me finished her song. It was my turn next, and I didn't know what to say. Compared to the others, my life was nothing. I worried if I spoke of my troubles, I'd offend them. I couldn't imagine what they'd been through. I felt them waiting for me, wondering what I would say. I opened my mouth, and all I could do was sing. The room was silent except for my voice, thin at first, then stronger and more assured. A kind of electricity was in the air, and a few minutes into my song, everyone started singing with me. I led the song, and the choir came in behind me in a swell of voices that nearly choked me with emotion. When we finished, everyone was quiet.

The president of the worship team spoke up. "Young girl, I don't know you, but you can sing. You have a talent."

I couldn't keep the smile from spreading across my face.

"Our group will be singing in front of the whole school tonight. Would you sing the song you just sang with us? I think everyone would like to hear your voice. We can put your song on the top of the list."

I couldn't believe what I was hearing. The president of the choir was inviting me to solo! And in front of the whole school. Excitedly, I nodded yes. In the space of a half an hour, my whole world had changed. Maybe I was not so lost here after all.

Later that evening the president introduced our choir and we walked in front of the assembly. I was in the first row. I gazed out at the many faces staring up at me. I was so nervous my hands began to shake. When the president gave me the microphone, I was trembling so hard that I couldn't remember the song I sang earlier in the prayer room. Someone in the auditorium coughed. I stood there, frozen, except for the microphone, wobbling in my shaking hand. A soft murmur rose from the crowd as the choir conductor approached me to take back the microphone.

I was about to apologize for being such a fool when out of nowhere I recalled the song and began singing. The whole choir came in behind me, and it was the most beautiful feeling I had ever experienced. I would not be able to remember much of my actual performance. Just the overwhelming feeling of being part of something larger than myself, something strong and pure. I knew without being told that the song was a success. When we were finished, everyone congratulated me. They told me they were so amazed by my voice! From that day, I became a member of the worship choir. I had found my voice after all.

Every weekend, I went home to visit my siblings. They were always so excited to see me. I would tell them stories about my life at school, and they would tell me what they had been doing at home. Boris had just started primary school, and little Bettina was in kindergarten. Fils had two years left of primary school, and was earning excellent grades. I told them some of the stories our mother used to tell us, and Boris and Bettina would lean into me the way I used to lean into our mother. I loved their closeness. With Fils, Bettina and Boris, I was completely relaxed. It was such a relief to be with people who knew me so well, with whom I'd never have to explain anything.

A year had passed in our father's care, and still things seemed to be going well. He was teaching at a local high school, and was still a student at the University. There was food on the table every day, he looked after my brothers and sister, and when I was home with them over the weekends we would all go to church on Sunday. Just as I was relaxing into our new life, just as I was beginning to trust it, everything fell apart.

One day, while I was home for the Christmas break, a long holiday that lasted nearly two months, my brother Fils brought a friend home from school. The boy was from a Hutu family. My dad's face changed while looking at the boy. He asked him about his parents and before the boy finished responding, my dad was out of his mind.

"Killer!" he screamed. "You're one of the Interahamwe!"

We had no idea why this boy's presence sent our father into such a rage. He crossed paths with Hutus everyday. We lived among Hutu neighbors. To our horror, Dad began chasing the boy and punching him. We ran after our father, trying to hold him back, but he was so much stronger than we were. He was stronger than all of us combined. The boy managed to escape through the front door, and we were left panting in the house, staring at each other with wide eyes, terrified of what had just happened and what our father might do next.

The episode with the Hutu boy was a turning point. It was as though the dark side of my father had been waiting to be let out all along, and now it had been set free. He began beating all of us, not every night but a few times a week. He would leave the house for days and when he returned, he would scream at us, telling us the boy my brother brought into our house belonged to the same family that had killed his brothers. Dad's mental state became so unraveled that even our neighbors became afraid of him. He was developing a reputation in Butare as a drunk and a bully.

By then Dad had finished his studies, and thankfully for him, he'd already been offered a new job in the Northern Provence where he was appointed the executive Director of the city of Gisenyi. Unhinged or not, my father was a very smart man. While it was a relief to him to leave Butare, my brothers, sister and I were devastated. It was perhaps the most painful move we'd ever made, we were going to leave our best friends behind. Gisenyi was a six-hour drive from Butare, and there was not even a discussion as to whether I'd remain at my current school. Because it was over the holiday, I didn't even get to say goodbye to my new friends in the worship choir. We were on the move yet again. We'd begun to trust our father, to truly settle in, but now we could see it had all been an illusion.

We'd never belong anywhere. We'd never have a real home. Once again, we would have to start a new life somewhere else.

Chapter Seventeen: The Adventures of Life

The city of Gisenyi was very beautiful, surrounded by high mountains, hills, volcanoes and Lake Kivu. My father had two good jobs: one as executive Director of the city and one as a professor in a highly ranked private university. The move to Gisenyi had a positive effect on him. He set about trying to make a fresh start with us. Some evenings he'd come home with special sweets or other foods he knew were our favorites. I recognized the gifts as small requests for forgiveness from a man who was too proud to share his feelings, and I felt sorry for him. He was working hard to make us happy, and on his good days his love could be so light-hearted and sincere, he made us feel like we were the only people that mattered to him in the whole world. In those moments, perhaps we were.

He spoiled us, giving us everything we asked for and more. In the evenings, he was quick to help us with our homework. He always read my poems and comment on them. He often added a discourse on the horrors of the Hutu killers. He had a talent for taking the most complicated problems and explaining them in a clear, simple way. When his love shined upon us, we flourished, but we were always aware that at any moment the light might go out.

Dad found us a wonderful babysitter, a young woman named Leonie, and she helped to keep our family balanced and on track. Dad put us, my siblings and me, in the nicest schools in the city. Because I was starting the school term late, there was no room for me in the dormitory at the nearest boarding school, which was about three miles away. The school promised my father they would have a room for me after two semesters, so for the time-being I walked to school from home each day.

Life felt exotic, like a fancy adventure. I worried it was too good to be true. While once again our family did our best to pick up the pieces and heal, our country was trying to move forward as well. A new government program called Gacaca was all over the news. Gacaca was a mechanism for legal redress for the victims of the Genocide, a kind of community-level truth telling and accountability hearing, designed to handle the overwhelming caseload. The newly instituted Gacaca system would work hand in hand with the regular court system, commonly referred to as the "classic" court system.

Given the massive number of crimes committed during the genocide against the Tutsis, survivors intent on seeing those responsible prosecuted faced a two-tiered system, which normally began with pre-trial Gacaca proceedings and was expected to end with a trial and judgment in the classic courts. I asked Leonie to explain it to me in simple terms, and she said it was a program in which the perpetrators would come in front of survivors and tell them how they killed their families and apologize to them as if it was just a simple mistake. It didn't sound very healing to me.

Like most Tutsi Survivors, my father hungered for justice for his family. One day he left to go to Gacaca for testimonies, but he never came back home. He returned two days later and told us he'd been working, but I sensed he wasn't telling us the truth. He was beyond tired, exhausted to the point of sickness. I noticed he was wearing the same clothes he had on the day he left. It was almost time for me to return to boarding school, but seeing my father in such terrible shape convinced me I needed to stay behind to look after my siblings. I suspected Gacaca was opening old wounds for my father and I had the terrible feeling something bad was about to happen. There were warning signs when my father was about to lose his mind.

He'd grow quiet and stop talking to us. Sometimes he'd stay out all night, coming back in the morning only to shower and leave for work. He stopped going to church. It had been a month since the Gacaca programs had started throughout the whole country. As a city Executive Director, my father had to attend Gacaca proceedings not just for his family, but also for others. Every day, my father went to the proceedings and listened to an unending list of horrors, from the mouths of those who had committed the atrocities. When it came to his own family, Dad didn't want to hear the details of how his family was killed; all he wanted was to find their bodies and bury them in a respectful way.

It had always tormented him that he and so many other survivors had never been able to give proper burials to their lost ones. I knew he saw it as an extension of his own failure to them, as a son, an uncle and a brother. But there was no way for him to locate the bodies without listening to the whole sordid ordeal of his families' torture and murders. I braced myself for the worst.

Finally the day came when our world fell apart again. It was almost a relief when it did. The whole neighborhood started talking about my father and what he had been doing around the city. He stumbled in and out of bars, cursing Hutus and chasing them. He screamed the names of his family members that had been lost in the Genocide, and sometimes spoke to them out loud, as though they were with him having a conversation.

I learned that during the Gacaca testimonies a witness revealed to my father terrible things about his family's deaths. Just as my paternal grandmother had feared when she sent my mother, Fils and me away from her home in the early 1990s–we would be the only blood of her family who would survive the mass killing.

On April 6th 1994, the first day of the Genocide took place in–Ruhengeri, situated in the northern province of Rwanda, where my grandmother lived. The Interahamwe killers' first visit that day was to her home, where they killed everyone who was there–all her children, grandchildren and her in-laws. Then they-burned all of the homes and forced her to watch. They told her that the pain she would endure from listening to the sounds of her dying children, and smelling the smoke from her burning house would be enough punishment for her to live with. She begged for her own death but they refused to kill her.

They left her there, listening to the screams of her youngest daughter Uwamahoro, as she was-thrown alive into a 16 foot deep hole in the ground we used as a toilet back then.

They cut her arms off so she could fit, and no one could help rescue her. A few days later, the witness said, he took pity on my grandmother and went back and offered my grandma what she wanted most-to end her life. He killed her by machete.

The witness said all of this in gruesome detail. He spoke aloud of how they tortured each member of the family and how they have begged for their lives before they die. He said all of these things not to apologies but to torture my father. I wanted to close my ears to the reports that swirled around me. How could any man be expected to hear such things, I wondered, and remain sane!

In the days that followed, my father was a man possessed. He came home and beat us and dragged us to Lake Kivu to drown us. He ranted about how dying was the only solution to get us out of this miserable world. Luckily, when he was drunk, he was easily distracted. Something else would catch his attention and we'd break free of his grasp and hide. Then, unexpectedly, his anger would melt into sadness and he'd weep, telling us how much he loved us and how he didn't want us to suffer as he had. In his presence, I went numb. I built a wall around myself that would not permit me to feel anger or sympathy for him. And when things got really bad, I no longer had the energy to feel. What energy I had left was spent on my siblings and ensuring their protection. I had nothing left to give to my father.

I will never forget what happened one night in particular when I was sleeping in the same room with Fils. I was 13 or 14 years at the time. I had a sixth sense about what was about to happen. It was the most terrifying thing I can remember from my childhood. Around 2:00 a.m., I was awakened by a strange sound. Fils snored softly in the bed beside me. I thought maybe I'd dreamt it, but no, there it was again, a sound like metal scraping metal, like hinges creaking. Suddenly light from the living room flooded the room, revealing the dark silhouette of my father in the doorway. He'd removed the door from its hinges. He was coming after us. Before I could scream, he picked me up and slammed me against the wall, knocking the wind out of me.

As I struggled to catch my breath, I heard him beating Fils, raining down punches on my brother's head and shoulders. It seemed unreal, like a terrible dream, but the pain was real. Fils and I bolted from the room, looking for anywhere to hide. My father chased us through the house until we escaped outside. It was cold, and we were only in pajamas, but anywhere was better than being trapped with our Dad inside the house. We eventually settled against a tree in the neighbor's yard, huddled back to back for warmth. In the morning, we waited for my father to leave the house, then crept back inside to get ready for school. Thankfully, Boris and Bettina had been left untouched. When I looked in the mirror, my eyes were swollen and my face was covered with blood.

As things grew worse, when I had no one to talk to, I'd go to a candy and sweets shop that was on my way to school. The owner of the shop had a public telephone, and I'd stop in the shop every day and dial my mother's cell phone number. It was the only number I had memorized in my whole life. Whenever I called, no one answered. My hope was that one day someone might pick it up, and maybe it would be someone who knew my mother, and maybe that person would come rescue my siblings and me.

"What's going on in that mind of yours, little girl?" the owner of the shop would ask me, as I replaced the receiver after another dead end call. I never answered. I'd learned to hide my feelings at a very young age. My mother had taught me how. Besides, I knew nobody cared how I felt. Explaining myself would be wasting my words on deaf ears. Even if my heart was about to burst, I would smile like nothing had happened.

I began writing my letters to God again, and making songs from them. I asked him why my mother had forgotten us. Singing was my only comfort when life became miserable. I was becoming more religious, but I wasn't faithful to any one church. My notion of God was fluid. I'd believe in anyone I thought could bring our mother back.

Sometime in April, Dad disappeared for a week and no one knew his whereabouts, then he showed up without warning in the middle of the night. He was determined to finish us. *This is it*, I thought. *This is how we die.* Fils and I ran from the house with Boris and Bettina, but it was so terribly cold. High in the mountains, the temperature dropped sharply at night. I knew we would freeze to death if we had to stay outside all night, so I went back in the house to collect blankets for my siblings. Once I was back inside, my dad locked the door behind me.

I screamed for Fils to run with the kids, that I would be fine. I ran to the kitchen, looking for a cupboard to hide in, but the spaces were too small. Then I saw a box half filled with charcoal, and an idea popped into my mind. I climbed into the box and covered myself with another box, so that my dad would think there was only charcoal there. The box reeked and the coals were so uncomfortable, but I grit my teeth and waited, breathless.

My dad's laughter boomed through the kitchen. A sick feeling washed over me, and I looked up to see dad staring down at me.

"My dear lovely daughter, you think you are hiding, uhh? Come on, I'm not going to do anything bad to you. You are my first-born. Come on, get out of that dirty box," he said.

I was covered in soot. My face and whole body looked painted black. Dad took my hand nicely, like he'd never done before, and helped me to my feet.

"Are you hungry sweetheart?" he asked, smiling at me like I was someone else.

I was so terrified; my thoughts were very far away. I thought this would be my last day on this earth. Inside my heart, I was ready, praying. *God please take me to heaven, the world is tiring me.* For the first time in my life I was not scared of death. I felt stronger than ever before. With my father holding my hand, we left the house and he led us to our neighbors' door. He started knocking. Our neighbors lived within a snack and drink shop. As it was late at night, the shop was closed and our neighbors were asleep. Dad knocked on their door again, first softly, then louder and louder, but no one answered.

He started yelling. "You Hutu people, how can you sleep while my daughter is hungry! Wake up or I'm going to burn this stupid house down like you did to my parents. I won't repeat it again. Open the door now!"

They finally opened the door, and I could see they were more afraid than I was. The neighbors gave me cookies and gave my father a Twelve-pack of beer. As we left, he called to them to wait up for him, because he might return for more drinks. Then he walked me home, humming as though nothing at all was wrong. We sat together in the living room, and he started drinking. He would continue to drink all night, and I stayed up watching him, tired and wary. Fils and the others had stayed outside all night. Somehow, they had survived the cold.

In the morning, I took a shower and went to school without having closed my eyes for a minute the night before. I stopped by the candy shop to call my mother, praying today would be the day she'd pick up. The phone rang and rang, and then a generic voice kicked in: "The number you dialed does not exist." I hung up. My deepest fear was that my mother was long gone. Maybe she'd sacrificed us to save her self and was living on the far side of the world. The owner of the candy shop was getting sick of me. He stopped greeting me and started rolling his eyes when I came in the mornings. I didn't care.

The days began to blur one into the other. I would go to the candy shop to make my call, then go to school, where I would sit alone and sing until it was time to go to class. Sometimes a few friends would sing with me, and these were rare happy moments. Afternoon was my favorite time of day. I'd go pick up my little sister Bettina and little brother Boris. I loved walking home all of us together. We would tell each other stories about our day and tease each other. Then I would tell them some of the stories I remembered from my mom, and sing the songs we all knew and loved.

When we got home, it was time for taking baths and doing homework, then dinner. We begged Fils to tell us his movie stories. We had no idea where he watched the films. They were always action movies, and he was so good at repeating everything he saw and pantomiming the actions. His body language and facial expressions communicated so many details. He was so convincing, we imagined we were watching the films ourselves. When he finished one movie, we'd ask him to start another, and we kept this up until we could no longer ignore it was nightfall. No one knew what the night would bring, what surprises our father would have in store for us. Fils and I shared a room, and Boris and Bettina shared another. I always made sure our rooms were locked before I went to bed.

One night Dad banged on our bedroom door, yelling for us to wake up immediately. I opened the door for my dad, and he knocked my head against the doorframe.

"What did I do?" I asked, holding the side of my face.

Dad pushed past me into the room, and he lifted Fils from his bed and threw him against the wall. Fils lay stunned for a moment then scrambled up from the floor and we ran together from the house. There had been no time to change or grab a sweater. We were outdoors in the freezing night air. Going back inside was not an option. I rubbed my arms, wracking my brain for a solution. Where could we go? Fils was only in his blue pajama shorts. He didn't even have a shirt on. I was in my nightdress. Dad had some distant family about three miles away. It was far to travel alone on such a cold night, but it was the only option I could think of. Maybe dad's family would help us. We needed to do something, fast. I prayed Boris and Bettina wouldn't open their door. I hated leaving them in the house.

"Fils," I said through chattering teeth. "Do you think we can make it to Eric's house?"

"If we run," he replied.

We set off down the road. It was nearly 2:00 a.m. Cold winds whipped across the lake and lashed our bare limbs. We ran as fast as we could, trying to warm up, but the cold was still unbearable. We ran until we were breathless, then walked as quickly as we could, then ran again. Dogs barked at us, and I worried they might chase us, but there was nothing else to do but keep going. No one could help us but ourselves. Every time I felt like stopping, I remembered Boris and Bettina, and I pushed myself to keep going. I could no longer feel my hands and a strange prickling sensation spread through my feet each time they made contact with the pavement.

Finally, we arrived. I knocked on the door, and someone opened right away, as though they had known we were coming and were waiting for us. I opened my mouth to explain when the people inside the house began shouting. They were furious with us for arriving in the middle of the night. Dad's cousin Eric, a very tall and skinny man, pushed his way outside, grabbing us by the arm and turning us around.

"You stupid kids," he said. "Your dad is worried sick about you. He has no idea where you are. What the hell were you thinking?"

"But, but..." I stammered. I didn't know where to begin, or how to explain. I was shaking so hard from the cold, it was difficult to speak. "You know him!" I blurted out. "You know what he does to us. I thought you'd understand!"

But he didn't want to listen to us. Eric rushed us back onto the street. He didn't even give us a sweater or any way to cover from the cold. He seemed more worried about our dad than he was about our safety. As though dad had been dying from missing us.

Eric and his friend marched us home. No one spoke. When we arrived back at our house, my father threw open the door, exclaiming, "My God, it's you! Thank God! I was so worried something might have happened to you." He leaned down and hugged us like our safety was his greatest concern. I was numb, inside and out.

Dad put on a dramatic show for Eric. "Thank you so much," he said over and over. "Please come in. You must be freezing!"

Eric and his friend followed us into the house. Dad scolded us for running away and sent us to our room. We climbed back into bed and listened to the sounds of the men talking and drinking in the living room. We knew the night was not over. As tired as I was, I knew I couldn't let myself fall asleep. The sounds from the living room grew more raucous. We heard the crack of beer cans opening, of the men laughing. It sounded like they were having a great time. My father sounded different too. Carefree, jovial. I strained to keep my eyes open, but the bed was so warm, so comfortable. The last thing I remembered was telling myself to stay awake.

Then, suddenly, he was in the room again, slapping my face and dragging me from bed. Fils crouched in the corner of the room, crying. When dad turned away from me and I was able to get my bearings, I saw the door of our room had been knocked down. I screamed for help, thinking maybe Eric and his friend hadn't yet gone far. But no one came to our rescue. I watched my father punch and kick my brother; then he turned to come back for me. I shrieked and flew out of the room. Somehow, I have no idea how, Fils and I managed to escape the house for a second time that night. My father was drunk, his blows were clumsy. At least these small mercies allowed us to get away.

We ran deep into our neighborhood and hunkered down in a half-constructed house with an outdoor toilet nobody used.

It was nearly five in the morning. We held each other, trembling. My hands felt something sticky and wet, and I didn't know if it was Fils's blood or my own. We sat there and waited for the sun to rise, for father to leave for work.

I prayed to God. *If you exist,* I thought, *bring back my mother. Prove to me that you exist. If you don't bring back my mother, we will die in that house.*

When the sun was high enough, Fils and I crept back to the house, being careful not to encounter anyone in the street. No one could see us, we had to preserve the family name. Silently, we entered the house and began to get ready for school like always. Thank God, Boris and Bettina were untouched. They emerged sleepily from their rooms. They said nothing, but I knew from their tired eyes, they hadn't slept much that night.

Fils and I dropped Boris and Bettina at school, and then encountered Eric's friend on the road. When I saw him, I felt nothing but rage. He'd come back to check on us, he said, but I knew he'd never help us. No one would. He gave me a strange look, like there was something wrong with me.

"How was your night?" he asked. "Is everything OK?"

The previous night, he and Eric hadn't even listened to me. They hadn't cared at all then, why now? I despised him.

"Everything is fine," I said brightly. "I'm late, I've got to get to class!"

He stopped me, taking my chin in his hand. "Are you sure everything is all right?"

"Of course."

"Then why do you have blood in your ears?"

My hands flew to my ears, where I felt the dried blood. "This is how I was born," I said and wriggled from his grasp. "Thank you for checking on us!" I called over my shoulder. "We are doing well!" I left him standing there, walking away as quickly as I could.

I thought about calling Mom's phone number again. A few months ago, I'd stopped trying it. I'd given up, but this morning I couldn't pass by the candy shop without trying it again. I was desperate. I held my breath as I dialed the familiar digits. The call didn't go through. I left the candy shop and kept walking to school. When I arrived, everyone looked at me like there was something wrong with me.

My friend Mugwa pulled me aside. She was my closest friend in Gisenyi. We'd shared many secrets together, but I'd never been able to tell her about my father.

"Dydine," she whispered. "What happened to you?"

I shook her off. "Nothing! Why?"

"Your face is swollen all over, and you have blood in your ear and in your eye. Did you even sleep last night?"

I said nothing, just stared at her. I heard my mother's voice in my mind: *You must never let others know. Act like everything is normal.* I was so exhausted, and I was tired of pretending. I opened my mouth, but no words came out.

"Come with me," my friend said. She grabbed my hand and took me to the bathroom.

When I looked at my face in the mirror, I was shocked. I'd had no idea how horrible I looked. It was as though another girl stared back at me. She looked frightened, exhausted and weary. It was clear she'd been beaten. I'd never thought I would look so bad. I honestly never thought I could be that girl. I tried to hold in my tears. I couldn't show my friend I was sad. *I refuse to cry!* I said in my mind, over and over again.

Mugwa held some paper towels in one of her pockets and tried to blot the dried blood from my ear. I snatched the wad from her hand, and began dabbing at the blood. "Haha!" I said, smiling. "I got in a fight with my brother this morning."

She looked at me like she didn't believe me, but neither of us said anything more.

Fils and me in Butare with our childhood friend Claire

Chapter Eighteen: Raised from the Dead

My friend Mugwa brought me a bottle of water and told me to wash my face. We walked together into class, and she tried to protect me from the prying eyes and questions of the other students. In hindsight, they probably all knew about my father. Gisenyi was a small town, and he'd made many scenes in public. Still, I felt I couldn't betray our family's secret. Inside I felt like crying, but outwardly I laughed everything off. "You know how little brothers can be!" I said.

We had a Math exam I couldn't miss, so I waited out the whole day, took the exam and left school at 4:30, like I always did, to go pick up Boris and Bettina. With the little ones, I couldn't fake my smile. I didn't have the energy to pretend I was OK. They looked at me with questioning, innocent eyes but I had nothing to tell them. My mind was far away from where we were. None of us talked all the way home. When Fils joined us, his face was swollen all over. I couldn't believe this was the life we were living. What was the meaning of life after all? I wondered. Why would anyone suffer like this for an entire lifetime?

When we got home, I tried to help Boris and Bettina with their homework but I couldn't concentrate. I stood up without saying a word and left the house. I walked all the way to Kivu Lake, flashbacks replaying in my mind of all the disappointments I'd encountered in life. I was no longer certain of my engagement with living. I saw the face of every person who had let me down. I thought back to the attacks in Rwamagana, I recalled my parents' wedding, the beautiful day that had been ruined. The only people who hadn't failed me were my brothers and sister, and I was beginning to wonder if I had the strength not to fail them. We needed each other to survive, but I was so, so tired of it all. I could no longer stand my life. As I arrived at the beach, I started talking to myself. I didn't want to live like this. I wanted to die.

I started crying harder as I drew closer to the water. I sat down and started thinking about all the reasons I had to end my life. I wondered, could I just let go? Could I be strong enough to put an end to my suffering? I thought about my siblings and all the duties my mom gave me before she left. I thought about all we went through together, bad times and good ones, and asked myself, *who will tell them stories, who will give them sweaters, or blankets when it's cold, who will rescue them from their own father? How will they feel after hearing the news of my death?*

Asking myself these questions, I felt so selfish. I couldn't think my way out. There was no solution. Finally, I fell asleep. I was so tired and the air from the lake was so cool and peaceful. I slept hard, a dreamless sleep I hadn't had in a long time. The next thing I knew, I heard a man's voice asking me to wake up. It was a security guard. It was almost 7pm, and no children were allowed to remain at the lake after this hour. It was widely known the lake wasn't safe for kids. Some parts of the lake had methane gas in it, and there were often accidents in the evenings. Signs in the lake told people where it wasn't safe to swim, but in the darkness it was harder to see the signs. If anyone swam into these contaminated spots, they would die almost immediately. The guard's job was to prevent this from happening.

The guard was furious with me. He told me to go home, then decided to accompany me part of the way. We walked together a few miles before he gave up and turned back. On my way home it started raining. I walked slowly, counting birds and cars, like I was wandering without any particular destination. I hated this thing called life. I wished something would happen to me that would take me away from this place, but no sooner did the thought cross my mind than I thought of my siblings and I asked for the courage to live a little longer.

By the time I reached our neighborhood, a thick, hard rain was pelting down. I took a quick detour into the unfinished house, where I threw up and cried in noisy, choking sobs. I knew no one could hear me there, so I let it all out. I screamed louder and louder to God, ordering him to change our lives. I felt like I was about to burst. Then I knelt down and looked up in the sky. There was no roof over the bathroom and I screamed louder and louder. All I wanted was to free myself.

When I was finally spent, I prayed to God to make me strong so I could return to the house and deal with whatever awaited me there. I asked God to give me hope. Eventually, I dragged myself to my feet and walked home on shaky legs. When I opened the door, my siblings rushed to my side. They'd been waiting for me, and I could see they were worried. They looked at me like I was a stranger. It was so unlike me to take off with no explanation. I walked past them and went directly into my room to sleep. They followed me, and sat on my bed and started telling me funny stories about what they did at school. I didn't feel like laughing, but I couldn't help myself. They were so sweet and silly.

We all fell asleep on my small bed that night. My dad never came home, so we had one night's reprieve. I was so grateful for that one night of tranquility and for the first time grateful for having survived both the genocide and my father. I watched my siblings sleep in peace and thought that I could do this and be there for them and I could do this for myself. Indeed, I had to embrace this life and even love it. If I did so there just might be "Embracing Survival".

After that evening, we began taking extra precautions against my father. We dressed for the next day and slept with our clothes on. We kept extra layers of clothing beneath our beds in case we needed to grab something quickly and flee into the night. I vowed we would be ready every night, no matter what Dad did to us. After our failed attempt at seeking help from Eric, I knew it was up to us to protect ourselves. I would never again risk asking someone else for help and making the situation worse.

Dad often disappeared for days, only to show up one night to fight. We learned how to deal with suffering, we learned how to be what other people expected us to be. We were children of the city's executive director. Doggedly, I tried my mom's phone number every day for weeks. She never answered. I wasn't even sure the line was working anymore. I began to give up hope that she was ever coming back for us.

She'd probably had enough and had decided to walk away from all of us - my father included.

One night my father's beating was especially harsh, and I could tell from the stares of the people I passed on the street the next morning that I looked bad. I was scared and jumpy. A car backfired on the street and I nearly had a heart attack. I'd almost passed the candy shop when a voice inside me told me to try the number one more time. I paused and looked through the window at the telephone. It seemed like it was calling out to me. I wasn't sure if I wanted to try the number or not. Something told me that I couldn't take the disappointment this morning. *You need to accept that she's gone forever*, I told myself. But the other voice in my head told me to try one last time. Without having made a decision, my feet steered me inside the shop.

The owner of the candy shop saw me and said, "Hello, you. Been a long time. Where have you been? Are you here to make your call? Come and take it!" He held out the receiver to me. I grabbed the phone from his hands and dialed my mother's number. It rang twice when someone picked up.

"Hello, who is this?" a familiar voice asked.

It took me a few seconds to respond. It was my mother!

I started crying, I couldn't believe it was finally happening. I could hear my mother's voice for real. I could not say a word, I just cried and the woman kept asking, "Who is calling?"

"Ma...?" I said, and I cried like a baby.

"Dydine, is that you? Where are you? I've been searching for you for days! Talk to me, be strong. Tell me where you are."

The owner of the candy shop came closer to me, clearly worried about having a crying kid in his store.

I wasn't able to speak, I had so much to tell my mother but I didn't know where to begin. It tumbled out in a torrent. "Ma, your children are covered in blood and wounds. Come take us away before it's not too late, or you'll be picking up their dead bodies!" Without waiting for a response, I thrust the receiver into the hand of the storeowner, whose mouth hung open.

I looked at him angrily. "I'll bring you your money for the call tomorrow!"

"No problem, no problem!" he said quickly. He couldn't believe a 14-year-old girl could say those words to whoever was on the other line. He was frozen. I wiped my tears and continued on my way to school. It didn't occur to me until later that I'd forgotten to tell my mother where we were.

I had a very long day; the hours were too slow to bear. I couldn't wait to tell my siblings that I'd spoken with our mother. The whole day I was in my own world. I couldn't focus on my studies. I started saying goodbye to all my friends, and they were so confused by my behavior. Somehow I knew this would be the last time I saw them. As this conviction grew throughout the day, I became more and more excited.

Mom hadn't forgotten us after all! She could come back for us. When I met Fils, Boris and Bettina after school, they could tell that something had changed in me. I waited to share the news, savoring my happy secret. I just looked at them and smiled. Finally, I could no longer stand to keep it in. "Who wants to hear my great story for today?" I asked. "Today's story is going to change our lives!"

They gathered around me and we came to a standstill in the road. Bettina danced on her toes. "What's your news? Tell us!"

"Today I spoke to Mom!" I said.

They looked at me like I was lying.

"I wouldn't joke about something like this. I spoke with her this morning!"

"Where? How? Is she here?"

"I know she'll be here soon," I said, and I prayed the words were true.

Boris and Bettina hugged each other, and Fils wore a quiet smile the whole way home.

When we entered the house, Mom was there, sitting in the living room waiting for us. We all jumped to her and we cried for a while, without saying anything. Emotions tumbled from us. We were so happy, but whenever we tried to ask each other's news, we'd dissolve into tears.

"Children, listen. I have something important to say and I need you to hear me," Mom said. "I didn't abandon you. I've been searching for so long. When we were in Butare, there were no plans to move anywhere. Your father never told me you were in Gisenyi, and when I returned to Butare, his friends had all graduated. No one could tell me where you'd gone. I've been frantic."

As the surprise of Mom's presence began to wear off, I noticed a stack of suitcases beside the door. "Mama, what is happening out here?" I said.

"We're leaving immediately. You're all coming with me. I'll never leave you again. From now on, nothing will separate us. The good and the bad, we will always face it together. There's a car outside waiting for us."

We all looked at each other and smiled through our tears, then we packed our things and left.

What a life! This was the beginning of another new chapter, and we had no idea what to expect. All we knew was that it would be better than what we were leaving behind. For the five of us, it was a blessing just to be back together.

Boris on the right, Sabra my childhood best friend with her little sister Sabaha who was Bettina and Boris's friend in Butare

Chapter Nineteen: Angry Girl

We packed everything we could in the car and left the city that very same day. We fell asleep snuggled together in the backseat. It was a three-hour drive to Kigali. We stopped at a friend of my mother's. His name was Kayumba, and he was an old friend who had been our neighbor when we were living in Kigali in the late 1990s. Kayumba's family knew everything we were going through, and they'd been hosting my mom since she came back to search for us. One of his children rushed to open the gate.

Once again, we had to start from scratch. Mom had nothing, not even a job or a place to live. Once again, we would have to get by on the kindness of others until we could stand on our own feet. I remember the first night at Kayumba's house, overhearing my mom in deep conversation with Claudette, Kayumba's wife, who asked my mom how long were we going to stay with them.

"Devota, we can't have you stay for long with four children. We have so many children too. It's too much. We have to figure out how to find you a small place for your family. We'll be there for you, we'll support you anyway we can, but this many people under one roof won't work."

Mom begged her to give us at least one week so we could figure something out. "We'll be out of your house as soon as we can. I understand how this is a burden to you." My mom was so sad and lost, she didn't fall asleep all night. Bettina slept in the same bed as my mother, and I slept beside them on a mattress on the floor. Fils and Boris slept down the hall, in the same room as Claudette's son, Bebe. My own sleep was restless, and every time I tossed and stirred in the night, I heard mother crying beside me.

The next day, I pretended I hadn't overheard Mom's conversation with Claudette. I pretended to be happy, because I knew if I revealed my anxiety, my sense of dread and fear of the future, I'd only make Mother's suffering worse. I wished I could grow up more quickly, so I could find a way to help my mum. If I were a grown up, I could get a job and help support the family. Just once, I wanted to see my mother rest and relax, without having to worry about what we would eat or wear, or where we would live. My heart was full of sorrow and tears flowed inside my heart. I remembered my mother's regret that I'd been born, and in that moment, I felt as though I'd somehow cursed my family. I wanted to die. Somehow, I was certain, this was all my fault.

The next morning we had a family meeting; we sat down and discussed what our next step would be. Mother wanted to listen to everyone, and all of us kids had to contribute ideas for what we thought could be done to solve the serious problems we were facing. Mom encouraged each and every one of us to work hard to come up with solutions. Every night, she made us update her on what we'd been thinking and what solutions we were coming up with. Once again, my lovely mother lost her smile. Life was bitter to her.

I tried so hard to think of an answer to our problems that would keep us all together, but the only solution I could come up with was to return to boarding school. I'd never enjoyed being away from my family, but I would force myself to make the best of it. With me gone, I figured mom would have one less person to worry about. When I told her my idea, I hoped she'd refuse to send me away. After all, she had said that from now "on we'd all be together, no matter what". But when I told her, I could see in her eyes she was relieved. It occurred to me that the idea had already crossed her mind, but she was waiting for me to volunteer to go myself. I tried to be generous and understanding of our situation. I resigned myself to the situation and set about trying to find a school that would accept me.

I would be in the second semester of my second year in high school. Finding a school that could take me proved difficult. I tried to find a school near my family, so I could check in on them more easily, but it was mid-semester and there were no openings anywhere. And of course my father wasn't around to pay the tuition, so I'd have to qualify for a scholarship, but I kept expanding my search area, until suddenly an idea jumped to mind. My dad used to have drinks with one of the high school headmasters in Gisenyi. I wondered if I could use my dad's name to call in a favor. There was no way I could ask my father himself. He didn't know where we were, and we intended to keep it that way. I asked my mother if I could borrow some money and take the bus to Gisenyi. It would be up to me to get myself in.

Thinking once again about my own schooling reminded us that Fils was only one year away from finishing primary school. Soon he too would be able to leave for boarding school. When mom looked into starting him at a local school, she was told he had to return to his school in Gisenyi to finish his semester, otherwise he would fail and have to repeat the entire year again. Primary school students in Rwanda had to sit for national exams in order to continue on to high school. There was no choice; we had to figure out a way for Fils to finish his studies in Gisenyi and sit for the big test.

The national exams always happened after the school calendar year, and it was up to us to find a place to live during the exam session. It would be a challenge to find Fils a place to stay during his last two semesters, and for the exam. We worked our minds, going through our limited options. Mom shocked us all when she turned up an old friend in Gisenyi who could host Fils for a while, possibly through the end of the academic year. I volunteered to take Fils back to Gisenyi with me so Mom could stay with Boris and Bettina. She was so surprised that we were grown up enough to come up with ideas that truly helped her. She hugged us with tears in her eyes.

"I can't believe you are helping me to think," she said. "I know we can do this. Because of your quick thinking, we're going to be all right. I'm so proud of you all."

She gave me two thousands Rwandan Francs, kissed me and wished me goodbye.

"Go find a school, study hard, there is nothing else I can give you. Your education will be the key to your success." She pulled me in for a final hug. "One last thing," she said, looking me in the eyes. "Don't ever get traumatized."

Fils and I left Kigali for Gisenyi. When we arrived at the house of my mother's friend, they immediately accepted Fils and agreed to host me for one night so I could seek out the new boarding school the next morning. Mama Bebe, the mother of the house, told me she knew what we were going through. I pretended I didn't know what she was talking about, but accepted her hospitality. When I woke the next morning, Mama Bebe was up as well.

"Are you leaving now?" she asked.

When I said yes, she looked me up and down.

"Is that all you have for school?" she asked me, staring at my small satchel.

"I'll be fine," I said, but she hugged me tight.

"You're coming with me," she said with such authority I dared not contradict her.

Mama Bebe took me to the market and bought me school materials and other items I might need as a boarder. I was so grateful, but too shy to express it. I'd been worrying about how I would pay for my school supplies. Mama Bebe paid for a taxi to take me to the school and wished me good luck. It was the first kind gesture I'd received from another person in so long. It utterly shocked me, that there might still be good people in the world who were willing to help you.

The school was unlike any place I'd seen before. Formerly a Catholic boys school, it was built by Europeans in the old colonial style. The buildings were outdated, but beautiful, clustered around a large Catholic church adorned with flowering bushes. The students had not yet arrived for the new semester, so the place was serene as a painting. I knew this was one of the best schools in Rwanda, a school for smart kids, and I steeled my nerves as I sat in the headmaster's office. I pretended I had an appointment and sat for hours in the waiting room, hoping he'd soon show up. People in the office seemed resentful of my presence. No one spoke a word to me except for one man who passed by me repeatedly and must have tired of seeing me sitting there.

"Little girl," he said. "What are you doing here? What are you looking for?"

I responded politely. "I'm waiting for the headmaster. I am Dydine Umunyana, the daughter of Laurent Kanamugire. You know, the executive director of the city? Yes, I was supposed to meet with the headmaster today."

I don't know where I got the guts, but I delivered my lines smoothly. Of course, I had no idea who the headmaster was, and I had no appointment. The only thing I knew was that he was an acquaintance of my father's.

My father's name seemed to impress the man. "Oh, the executive's daughter!" he exclaimed, his face brightening. "I'm so sorry that you had to wait this long. I'm going to let him know that you are here and waiting for him. Just a moment," he said, and he hurried away.

After he told me that, I became even more nervous. I had no idea what to tell the headmaster if I did actually get to speak with him. The man came back to me, looking nervous. "I'm sorry, but the headmaster doesn't have anyone scheduled for a meeting with him today." I tossed my head, as though I were being terribly inconvenienced. "I've been waiting for hours," I said.

"Please tell him I'm his friend Laurent's daughter and I have an important message for him."

The man eyed me warily, as though trying to assess whether I was legitimate. I held my breath. Finally he sighed and went back to try again.

I was terrified when moments later, the headmaster himself came out to greet me.

The headmaster ushered me into his office and offered me the seat before a great wooden desk, strewn with books and papers. Sports awards and trophies lined the walls. The school was known for the success of its sports program. He took a seat behind his desk and I told him why I was there and what I wanted. I told him my father was supposed to have come with me today but he was tied up with a very important project.

"He admires your work with your students. He definitely wants me to attend your school," I said. Then I showed him my previous school reports.

He smiled as he reviewed my grades. "I knew you were smart like your dad.

Tell me," he looked up. "Do you do well in Math? You are a mathematician's daughter."

"I'm just OK," I said. "I'm not like my father."

The headmaster closed my school report and folded his hands on his desk. "Any school could be yours, my dear. We're all looking for students like you. Come back tomorrow with all your school materials, and your mattress. We will show you to your class. Welcome to College Inyemeramihigo!"

My heart spilt all over the place. I couldn't think where to go or what to do. I was elated he would accept me, but I had no mattress and nowhere to go before tomorrow. I thought quickly.

"Actually, I forgot to tell you another thing."

The headmaster had already returned to the stack of papers on his desk. At my words, he looked up, surprised.

"My father told me that you would take care of my mattress and supplies.

He was hoping you'd take me now so I could stay overnight tonight."

I forced my face and shoulders to relax as my heart raced wildly.

The headmaster paused. He seemed thoughtful, amused. I waited desperately for his answer.

Finally, he smiled. "I think you will be my favorite student this year. You're the only student I've met who wants to start studying early."

He stood and gestured for me to follow him. We walked to the girls' dormitories, where he introduced me to the girl's leader and asked her to help me choose a dorm and a bed.

"Umunyana," he called to me, as he was walking away. "After you're done with your accommodations, please come back to my office. I'll complete your registration and will have your school materials ready." He arched an eyebrow. "I'm sure your father will pay me back."

"Yes, of course." I nodded emphatically, knowing that would never happen.

True to his word, the headmaster gave me everything I needed, and that night I went to sleep in the dormitory for the first time. I couldn't believe my good luck. I'd done it. I'd taken my fate into my own hands. When classes began in the morning, I realized all the students already knew each other. I was the only new student arriving in the middle of the year. Everyone asked me why I was changing schools, even my new teachers. They all asked me to stand up and introduce myself and say why I was here. I told a different story every time.

Most of my fellow students came from wealthy backgrounds. They had plenty of spending money and were always buying snacks and pens from the store on campus. I began to hate them. I didn't see how we could ever relate to each other. I started becoming angry at everyone and everything. I didn't want to do any of the normal things the other kids were doing. I didn't want to be like them. They only wanted to party and thought I was weird for staying in and studying or sleeping.

I wasn't the only odd man out. There were some other students who came from modest backgrounds. They were scholarship kids, children who had been orphaned or who had no one looking after them. It wasn't long into the new semester when I discovered that some of the female students were selling their bodies to rich old men in exchange for gifts. These men were known as "Sugar Dads," and I hated them. The girls laughed about it, and thought they were the ones in charge. From their perspective, they were manipulating the old men to fund their basic needs, such as school materials, pocket money, and other frivolous gifts. I saw right through it. The men were using these vulnerable young girls for sex.

One of my closest friends at school was one of the students prostituting herself in exchange for gifts. Just a few months after we met, she was diagnosed HIV positive. Before her diagnosis she had already gone through the gifts and money she'd received. Her short-lived instant gratification led to a lifetime of regrets.

"Oh, Dydine," she would say to me. "if only I'd known."

As in years past, my only comfort was singing with the church choir. Sometimes it felt like the only thing that could distract me from hateful thoughts. I discovered I couldn't read and absorb material with any kind of recall. My mind would wander to other things, namely to the other students from Hutu families, and how much I hated them because they hadn't suffered as I had. I became so negative about everything. My thoughts became my prison. I blamed everyone in my life including my own mother. The only person I didn't blame was God. The littlest thing could set me off. What I loathed most were the questions from my fellow students. "Do you have parents?" someone might ask. "You seem like an orphan. You never talk about your family." In hindsight, the person asking likely was trying to befriend me, but I viewed all such attempts to get to know me with hostility.

After a few months at school, I started having stomach problems. I was frequently sick, and headaches became a daily occurrence. I began spending several days a week at the infirmary, instead of in class. I never called my mother, because I knew she likely had enough to deal with, and I didn't want to be just one more burden. The semester lasted three months, but for me it felt like an eternity. Finally, I was headed back to Kigali with Fils for the Christmas and New Years holidays. He had successfully completed his exam.

When we arrived in Kigali, Boris was waiting for us. He walked us home to our new house. He was so silent, Fils and I worried something was very wrong. I peppered him with questions. "How's life? How's your new school? How is the new house?"

"I'm not telling you anything," he said to me. "Mom told me not to."

The entire way to the new house, we tried to convince him to catch us up, but he said nothing at all. Suddenly, he stopped at a beautiful green gate. He gestured to us to go in.

"Wait," Fils said. "We live here?"

I was tired and losing my patience. "Boris, stop playing games! We want to go home."

Boris laughed. "It's not a joke! This is home, this is where we live now."

Fils and I looked at each other, then burst into laugher. We rushed inside, but once we'd entered the compound we could see two houses, one extremely small and the other quite large. Our smiles faded. We knew for sure the small house must be ours.

Mom came out and hugged us and showed us where to put our luggage. The house was so tiny, it only had one room. We tried hard to hide our disappointment.

"What do you think?" Mom asked.

"It's really nice," Fils said.

"It's so beautiful," I added lamely, hearing the lie in my voice.

Boris, Bettina and Mom began giggling and then their giggles turned into full-blown laughter. Fils and I looked at them like they'd all gone mad.

"You should see your face!" Mom pointed at me, laughing. "Trying so hard to stay positive." She came and wrapped her arms around me. "This is the kitchen house, Dydine. We live over there, in the big house." She pointed to the large house across the way, and I could scarcely believe it.

"Welcome home!" Mom said, ushering me through the doorway of the big house and throwing on the lights.

I walked my eyes all over the house. I'd never lived in such an elegant place. The entry opened into a sizable living room with a powder room and a large bedroom. It looked so clean and comfortable. Following my nose, I wandered into a dining room where a nice dinner was ready and waiting for us. Mom told me and Fils to go shower, and then we sat down to dinner.

"Mom, how did you get this house?" I asked, worrying it was too good to be true.

"Haha! God looks for the poorest and to them he does not close his eyes," she said. "A week after you left for school, we moved into the small house for a few months. Two single guys lived in this house, and when they saw me and the kids, they felt bad about the conditions we were living in. They decided to move and they gave me the large house for the same price I was paying for the small one. So, here we are!"

When Fils and I talked about our lives at school and the challenges we faced, Mother cried and smiled at the same time. When dinner wound down, She said she had something important to tell us.

"We need to work together in this life if we're going to make it. Sometimes we won't have enough to eat, we may not even have the comfort of knowing where we'll sleep, but we will live, and trust me, we're going to make it if we stick together." We all looked at her and smiled.

"I'm serious!" she said, laughing. "I know I repeat myself, but I'm serious. We need each other. Never forget that. Now who wants to watch some TV?"

Chapter Twenty: Single Mom Survivorship

Our time in the beautiful big house in Kigali lasted almost three years. It was a time of conflicting emotions. Mom still couldn't find a job, and she routinely missed the rent. Fils and I returned to school (Fils was now in high school as well), and Boris and Bettina were still too young to be of much help. Life was very difficult for Mom. She started selling our belongings to pay for food, school fees and supplies. After eight months of missed rent payments, our landlords' generosity wore thin and they threw us out.

After that, we skipped around to different houses, most of which had just one room for all of us. We had nothing but each other, and although many days we went without food, we children were happier than ever before. We slept well at night. We were together. Our nomadic life became a kind of game to us. We'd get kicked out, and then the hunt would be on for a new place to live. If we adapted to these conditions, my mother never did. These were degrading circumstances for someone with so much pride.

My mother insisted we put up a brave front to the rest of the world. We were always to look clean and presentable, even if we were down to our last outfit. We were never to let anyone know the truth about our father. We were to be happy and nice no matter what was happening in our family. She led by example, always applying makeup before she left the house, still wearing her red lipstick for special occasions. She sold most of her clothes and jewelry, but she made certain she always looked put together. She couldn't afford to buy fresh flowers anymore, so when we were out and about, we'd always be on the lookout for wildflowers to bring home. What little we had, we made the most of it.

As time wore on, Mom's impatience with our condition began to spill over to us. Her anger returned, and once again we became fearful around her. She would cut us down for the slightest mistake. She hated holidays, because it meant we'd all be back at the house, and she'd have more mouths to feed. She developed the habit of mumbling as she wandered through our house, blaming us for her miserable life. Under her breath she'd mutter that her life would have been so different without us. Of course, it was painful to hear her say such things, but there seemed to be nothing we could do to cheer her. She was still so young, in her 30s.

My relationship with my mother had worsened as I grew order. I wasn't a child any longer and I hadn't been for a long time. And yet, she ordered me around as though I were no different from Boris or Bettina. I felt the unfairness of her rebukes, and sometimes I'd have to turn away to hide my anger. I missed the days when my love for her was simpler.

Compared to our father, she had been like an angel sent to protect us. Her presence, which was once such sweet relief and provided such a sense of security, was now its own source of negativity. I tried to be compassionate and understanding, but I felt my own patience wearing thin. Sometimes it seemed our only happy moments as a family were when we all watched TV together and could take a break from our everyday struggles.

Mom sold most of our stuff but she never sold our TV. TV was our distraction. When she had no food to put on the table, Mom turned on the TV. She wanted our eyes to look at the TV instead of at her, because she knew there was nothing she could do when our eyes asked for food, our hunger written plainly across our faces.

Luckily for her, we all loved TV. Each of us had a favorite program. Boris was so smart, always the first in his class, and he loved CNN, BBC, FRANCE 24 and National Geographic. Fils loved everything about sports, while Bettina and I watched the telenovelas and movies on Telemundo. Oprah was mother's favorite show. It aired on Rwanda television at 10pm at night. We weren't allowed to stay up so late on weeknights, so Mom would only let us watch Oprah on the weekends. We used to beg her to stay up late and watch with her, but she was firm and disciplined. We may not have had food, but we had structure. She was nothing if not well organized.

Boris came up with an ingenious way for us to trick our mother so we could stay up late and watch Oprah. He knew she loved getting her feet massaged, so he'd offer to give her a foot rub fifteen minutes before Oprah was supposed to air, knowing well she'd fall asleep five minutes into the massage. Bettina and I caught on and would offer to give Mom head massages because she always had migraines, and for a few brief moments, Mom would seem like the happiest woman in the world. She would fall asleep with a smile on her face, and we'd be able to watch the whole show while she snored softly from her armchair. Once the show ended, we'd wake her up and tell her it was so late, we wanted to go to bed. She'd thank us for the massage and wish us goodnight.

We got away with this for several months before she caught on to us. She'd picked up on the fact that when she needed a massage and asked for one at other times of the day, no one would offer her one. From then on, whenever we'd offer her a massage, she'd decline and off to bed we'd go.

One night in 2007 when she was watching Oprah by herself, Mom woke us all from sleep.

"Dydine! Fils! Wake up. Come quickly, I want you to see this!"

We ran into the living room.

"Look," she said, pointing at the TV. "This woman had a husband like your dad, but now she and her son are so happy."

The episode she was watching mirrored our own lives. The show was about a man who beat his wife violently; unbeknownst to him, their son filmed him while he was beating his mother and sent the footage to Oprah. Now the mother and son were both guests on Oprah's show, bravely sharing their story with the world. They were articulate and nicely dressed.

"See," Mom said, "we might be suffering now, but the time will come when our lives will change. You'll all have a better life someday. What we're going through now is temporary. It will make us stronger."

We sat down with her and watched the entire show. It only reminded me of everything I wanted to forget about my father. I hated anything that made me remember those terrible nights. I couldn't sit still any longer. I stood up.

"Where are you going?" Mom asked me.

"I'm tired, I'm going to bed," I said. Once I was alone, all I could do was sit down and cry. Mom always promised miracles, but just when something was going right for us, it seemed calamity would strike again. Even without the threat of dad's abuse, we were still so far from being OK.

Life had to continue no matter what. Time passed and I'd completed my first three years of high school. In Rwanda, it's customary to change schools for the last three years of high school, so I confronted a new beginning yet again. At my new school, I needed all new materials, but my mother had no money to buy me anything. I was a teenager; I didn't understand it. I was furious with her that I'd have to show up the first day of school without even a new notebook. The other students, even the professors, would judge me.

"You have to help me!" I wailed. "I won't go unless you help me!"

Selfishly, I wanted her to give me everything she had. I didn't care that she needed the money to support my other siblings.

"Of course you're going!" Mom yelled back. "Don't be so proud, Dydine. Besides, I can't afford to care for you if you stay. You're going and that's final!"

When we walked to the bus stop together before my first day of class, we didn't speak. When the bus finally arrived, Mom looked at me and said, "Darling, I love you. There's nothing more I want in the world than to give you everything you need. But I can't do that now, and you have to help me by understanding. If you don't try to understand, your siblings never will. They look up to you."

She hugged me so tight then it caught me off guard.

"One more thing," she said, wiping a tear from her cheek. "Don't ever get traumatized. I don't want you ending up like your father. I can't stand to lose you as well."

By this time she was crying openly. Embarrassed, I wriggled free from her embrace and boarded the bus. Tears flowed down my cheeks as I took my seat, but they were tears of anger, not sadness. I was furious with my mother. She was all pretty speeches. Maybe I would get traumatized, just to spite her. Maybe I'd let all the anger and shame I felt build up until I burst open and there was nothing left of me. At least there was one good thing about going away to school, I thought. I wouldn't have to be around her anymore.

An old man across the aisle observed me for a time, then came closer and said, "It's been a very long time since I've seen that kind of love between a mother and child in this country. You just made my day. You've shown me that one day our people's hearts will feel again..."

He kept on going and going, and I wanted to punch him in the face. I fixed him with a blank stare but he wasn't getting the message. I waited for him to finish and leave me alone, and when he wouldn't I turned away to look away out the window. It was a two hour drive from home to my new school, in the Southern Province of Rwanda.

Chapter Twenty one: The Evil Headmaster

When I arrived at school, I went to the office to register for classes and there I met my new headmaster. He was a strange looking man, with a bald head, stooped shoulders and a high-pitched voice. He wore a long khaki coat and carried a stick, which he shook in my face when he asked me to repeat my name. I told him my name several times, and each time he seemed to grow angrier and he yelled louder for me to say it again.

I wasn't mumbling, and I wondered whether he might be hard of hearing. *Was there something wrong with my name?* I wondered. Little did I know, that this man was about to make my life miserable. He hated me from the very first day. I was baffled by his reaction to me. Whenever he'd see me in the halls, he'd go out of his way to yell at me, always shaking his stick, sometimes making up rule infractions that seemed to apply only to me. I tried to dodge him, and sometimes when I saw him coming, I'd turn and run the other way. Once, he caught me and tripped me with his stick. I went sprawling on the floor of the hallway, and as he passed by me he yelled at me to watch where I was going and to be more careful.

I wasn't used to being disliked, and so I tried to find a way to please him, to prove him wrong about me. When I heard he was fond of singing, I sang a song when he passed by me in the hallway on the way to dinner one evening. He slowed and stood before me. He began to speak and I was certain he was about to compliment me. Everyone had always complimented me on my singing. "You," he said, jabbing his stick three times into my shoulder. "You remind me of a former student who had a particularly bad attitude. I'm watching you," he said, and walked away.

I wasn't ready to give up my quest to win over the headmaster. I asked my friends what they thought I should do, and they suggested I go to church, because the headmaster was a Catholic religious man. When I went, instead of letting me pray with the other students, the headmaster told me to go clean the church entrance. I did as I was instructed, but came away with the impression that my obedience had infuriated him even more. One day at school, a few of the student leaders organized a performance in which different students would sing and dance and do short skits. The show was scheduled for that same evening, in front of the entire school.

"Dydine, you must sing!" one of my friends said. "You can show the headmaster you're nothing like he thinks you are. He can't possibly hate you after he hears you sing."

That's what I'd thought too, but I was too embarrassed to tell them about my previous encounter with the headmaster in the hallway. Maybe a real performance would do the trick. I'd pick my best song and practice it until it was perfect. He'd have to listen to me until it was over, and then he'd know he misjudged me.

That night, I made certain my uniform was clean and pressed. I took extra care with my appearance, and when it was my turn I nervously took the stage. I closed my eyes and began to sing. When I opened them, I scanned the amazed faces of my friends in the audience. I could tell from their expressions they were enjoying my song. But when my eyes landed on the headmaster, sitting erect in his seat in the front row, I saw him scowling. Even from the stage, I could see him gripping his stick so tightly his knuckles were white.

From that day forward, things grew worse for me. The headmaster treated me like his personal slave. Any time anything needed cleaning, he'd pull me out of class and put me to work. The dirtier the job, the happier he was. He was never satisfied with my efforts. If I scrubbed the floor of the toilets, he'd come in and cluck as he stood over me and tell me to clean them again. He humiliated me in front of my friends. I began to suspect the headmaster had genocide ideologies. I thought back to my first day at school when he asked me over and over to repeat my name. Did he know my father? I wondered.

The first holiday I returned home, I told my mother I needed to change schools. She was in the bathroom, applying makeup in the mirror. I fiddled with her lipstick tube, until she took it from my hands and expertly swept the lipstick over her lips.

"The headmaster hates me," I said. "I'll be better off somewhere else."

I didn't expect her to care. After all, she'd yanked me out of more schools than I could remember when I was a child. It never seemed to worry her then.

Mom sighed. "I can't let you do that, Dydine," she said, picking up a tissue and blotting her lips once. "You've been changing schools all your life, but only because of our family's circumstances, not because of any difficulty you faced. You're a fighter, Dydine, and if you let one person chase you away from school, you'll regret it." She wadded up the tissue and tossed it in the trash, then reached for her eyeliner.

I seethed. How dare she talk to me about being a fighter? I'd been fighting for my survival since I was three years old. I tried to keep calm. I didn't want to tangle with her. I'd learned by now that it was almost impossible to win an argument with her. I just wanted her, for once, to try standing in my shoes.

"Why can't you ever take my side, mom? It's like you want me to suffer. You have no idea what I'm going through."

She stopped applying the eyeliner and turned from the mirror to look at me directly for the first time.

"I do care, Dydine. No matter what you think. You're studying for yourself and your future, not for me and not for any headmaster. Don't ever let any one person break you down."

"Like Dad broke you down?" I said.

For a moment we stared at each other in shock, both of us surprised by what I'd said. Mom and I never talked about Dad. Since she'd given up hope of us reuniting as a family, his name was painful to her. I knew she saw her inability to heal him as a personal failure. I couldn't believe my nerve, and I braced myself for the slap I knew was coming. Mom never tolerated back talk. I decided I didn't care. It was worth it. I could do the same thing to her. But the slap never came.

Her expression changed as she looked at me, as though she were realizing for the first time how much I knew and how much I'd seen. It seemed to sadden her. I stared into her face, still so beautiful, her fine features thrown into sharper relief by the makeup. She reached toward my face and I flinched but she simply laid her hand against my cheek.

"You're going back to school, Dydine," she said, and left the room.

Since the Genocide, the government had designated the month of April as a time of remembrance. Everyone in the country, every institution and school, had to commemorate the massacre through a series of programs designed to support the survivors. I hated April. Rather than being a time of healing, it only dragged up awful memories. Every April, we were made to relive those terrible hundred days of chaos. My fellow students reacted differently. For the Hutus, it was a time of shame and confusion.

Those who attended high school with me were far too young to have participated in the atrocities, but their parents and grandparents had, unless they were from moderate Hutu families. I wondered what it was like for them to be forced to acknowledge their families were murderers. Outwardly, they seemed guilty and ashamed, although I wondered if inwardly they were defiant. It was taboo to talk about, but Hutu/Tutsi violence wasn't exactly a thing of the past. There were still crimes. Sometimes I think we liked to pretend we'd all evolved and learned from the tragedies, but everyone carried their hidden prejudices.

During April, most of my fellow survivors were traumatized all over again. My school gave these students permission to go home and come back after the commemoration. Sometimes I wanted to go home too, but my mother's voice was always in my head, reminding me, *don't you dare get traumatized.* If I showed up at home, I knew she'd send me straight back. Giving in to the dark thoughts and memories that swirled in my mind that April was not an option. I imagined the second part of my mother's sentence, the one she left unsaid, *Don't you dare get traumatized. If you do, I'll give up on you, just like I did on your father.*

Once again, singing became my refuge. I had kept up my story writing and still loved creating new songs. Most of the songs I composed were songs of sorrow. During breaks, my friends would ask me to sing for them. I would close my eyes and just start singing like no one was there. Some of my friends loved singing too, and I had the idea to start a worship team at school. Everyone loved the idea and very quickly after the club was created, dozens of students, ones I knew and ones I did not, all joined up. I thought the headmaster would love the worship team. He was always shaking his stick at us and telling us to be leaders, to take initiative. But when he found out I'd started the team, he became furious.

He called me into his office one morning. "This is a Catholic land. I won't tolerate any other religious group on the premises."

It was true that our school was located in a part of Rwanda that was largely Catholic, but Rwanda was not a Catholic country. Many other forms of Christianity, Islam, Jehovah's Witnesses and other religions were practiced here in Rwanda as well. I didn't particularly care what religion my fellow students were. I just wanted to sing. I stood obediently with my head down and let the headmaster berate me.

Then I left his office and just kept doing everything the same as I had been. When the headmaster found out the choir hadn't been disbanded, he went crazy. He stormed into our practice room and moved out all the chairs by himself, tossing them outside, where they clanged loudly against the floor. We watched him, incredulous. It wasn't often we saw an adult throw a tantrum. Some students giggled, covering their mouths with their hands. By now, everyone knew of his hatred for me. It had become a kind of joke around the school.

"You are not allowed to be here!" the headmaster yelled. "You are the wrong religion!"

When he'd thrown the last chair, he stood panting, looking around at the crowd which had grown to watch him. He attempted to straighten his posture, pulled out a handkerchief and wiped the sweat from his face and bold head. He coughed, twice, and shouldered his way through the students, heading back to his office.

I began to hate school, but my mother pushed me so hard, I knew I couldn't quit. Deep down, I knew she was right: my education was the only thing that could change my situation in life. I had to do well. It was confusing though, when the same people who were supposed to teach me seemed to want me to fail. I knew I wasn't the only student the headmaster went after. He never came out and said anything directly, but I noticed most of the kids he hated were Tutsi. All my friends agreed the problem was with him and not with me.

One afternoon that April, two of my friends and I were sitting in a classroom, taking a break. It was a sunny day, and warm rays poured through the windows onto our backs. We lay with our heads down on our desks, exhausted. It had been a long night of taking traumatized genocide survivor students to the hospital. So many students had nightmares and flashbacks, and sometimes it seemed impossible to wake them. You had to be careful not to shake them or startle them, because they couldn't tell the difference between reality and their dreams or flashbacks, and sometimes they lashed out and tried to fight you.

The headmaster walked into the classroom and rapped his stick on one of the desks. We shot up in our seats. He scanned our faces, searching for something wrong with us, something he could criticize. Then he spotted a broken window in the corner of the classroom. Shattered glass still lay across the floor. I hadn't been there to witness it, but the rumor was a traumatized student had had an episode and broken the glass earlier that week.

"Umunyana!" the headmaster called to me in his high, shrill voice. "I say, clean up that broken glass. When I come back, I want the window completely fixed!"

His request was absurd. I could sweep up the broken glass, but we both knew that maintenance would have to order a new window to replace the old one. There was no way I could fix it myself. Something inside me gave way. I no longer had any desire to please this man, to make him like me. I despised him, and I realized I didn't care if he knew it. I looked up at him, directly into his eyes, and held his gaze. We said nothing, but into that look I poured all my bitterness and frustrations. The longer I held his gaze, the more nervous he appeared.

I watched his bony Adam's apple bob in his throat as he swallowed. He set his stick down on one of the desks and approached me. Standing closer, he began to ask me once again to clean up the broken glass, but in a kinder, gentler voice. Something in my expression stopped him mid-sentence. I could tell he was startled I hadn't jumped to do his bidding. I'd always listened to him before. Everything he asked me to do, I did. His presence had terrified me, but I wasn't terrified anymore. Something like fear flickered across his face, and without another word he exited the room.

That night, he called my friends in to meet with him in his office. He asked them what had happened to me. *What's going on with her? Is she all right? Is she traumatized?* He apologized to my friends for his behavior, but not to me. He'd found out who had broken the window, he said. It was one of the student survivors, who had broken the window the previous night and fled. The student was still missing and no one knew whether he was safe or not. *If I'd known it was the other student, I never would have scolded Dydine*, he said.

My friends nodded but kept quiet. When he pressed them, they told him they had no idea what was wrong with me. *She must be traumatized*, he said. He gave my friends some money to buy some water, which was what was commonly done for those who were traumatized, and told them to make sure I got to bed safely. When my friends came to tell me about the meeting, they were giddy and excited.

"You showed him, Dydine!"

"Yes, you taught him a lesson!"

"Now maybe he'll respect other people. We're so proud of you, girl."

My friends congratulated me, and I was happy to be their hero for five minutes, but I felt like a shell of myself, drained of energy and the will to make any effort. Maybe I was traumatized after all.

The next day, I smiled like always, but inside I hurt. The students who were traumatized were treated like they were crazy, but I knew now they weren't crazy. They were wounded. The sadness had simply become too much to bear. My heart was trying to understand things I'd refused to think about for years, and I didn't know how to express this to my friends. It became easier to avoid them than to be together making small talk. Even when I was surrounded by other people, I felt incredibly lonely.

The feelings grew until I was incapable of pretending anymore. My brave façade crumbled. I complained about my life to anyone who would listen, about everyone and everything that had let me down. I became the sad person my mother always told me no one wanted to be around. At first I thought once I let everything out, I'd heal myself, but I found that the more I complained, the more my negative thoughts multiplied. It felt good to let go and give in. It was so much easier to be angry.

Chapter Twenty Two: Healing That Shapes Our Future

A few months later, the school administration removed the headmaster and accused him of having Genocide ideologies. There had been so many complaints from students and their families, and the administration realized that all the students the headmaster had singled out for punishment were Tutsi survivors. My worst fears about the headmaster were confirmed. He hated me because I was a Tutsi survivor and he was Hutu, and he wished I'd never survived the Genocide.

I was home on break when he was ousted, and did not learn the news until my fellow students and I returned to campus. It was exciting news that the evil headmaster was gone forever, but learning the reason why made me feel more sad than triumphant. We would meet our new headmaster at assembly on Monday morning, and the rumor was he was the complete opposite of the headmaster who came before him. I gathered the worship team and together we wrote out a plan, asking the new headmaster to let us sing and pray at school.

At the assembly, I studied the new headmaster from my seat. He was tall and very slender and looked to be in his early thirties. He spoke softly and had an easy laugh. His energy was so calm. I wanted to like him, but I was wary. I met with him for the first time when I pitched him my proposal for running the worship choir. He seemed impressed both by my idea and my level of confidence in the meeting.

The next day, he invited me and my group to meet with him to discuss how the school could best implement our proposal. I was astonished when he singled me out.

"Your colleague Dydine has shown great leadership, and I believe her talent and intelligence will make this one of the most successful groups at the school."

My face flushed, and I looked away, embarrassed but secretly proud.

"This proposal is approved," the headmaster said, "and Dydine will be the leader of your group."

I practically floated out of his office, and true to the headmaster's words, my group became a great success.

I threw myself into my writing and singing more than ever. It was my outlet to express all my pain and sorrow. Sometimes I thought about writing books. I wanted to write fiction, but each time I'd get a few pages into the writing, I'd realize I was writing about myself and the story of my family. Something about this scared me, and I'd stop and tear up the papers.

One day, I came up with an idea for a book titled *The First Born*. It began like a poem:

Sometimes we are born accidentally. Sometimes we die even before we are born. Sometimes we are born from so much love.

But most of the time, our births are a reminder of change, which is constant in life. Our lives might be changed by the miraculous, or they might be changed by nightmares.

Sometimes we become responsible before our years, and we skip ahead past our childhood.

Sometimes we grow up in the hands of our grandparents, believing they are our parents. We call our cousins our sisters and brothers, and our aunties and uncles our parents as well.

But time after time we go on to become something, because we think big. We are proud of what we've survived and what we've accomplished.

Sometimes the consequence is the hatred of our mothers. We cause them problems without knowing why.

Or maybe we will bring light to our mothers' lives, and no one will be more wonderful in their eyes than we.

Sometimes, we think we are the first born, but trust me, we never know. That's the first-born.

I remember sharing these first lines with one of my friends, and the first thing he asked me was what inspired me. His question made me so uncomfortable, I stopped writing the book. I wasn't ready to explain anything to anyone.

Then, days later, I would start over again, trying to find some way of separating my writing from my own story. My past was like a magnet that kept pulling me in, even as I struggled to break away.

Our worship team became well known in the school, and everyone knew me as its leader. One night I was going to sleep when I heard a boy calling my name through the dormitory window.

"You in there!" he said. "Please let Dydine know the Headmaster wants her to attend a special meeting of student leaders tonight. It's very important!"

I was curious, so I rose from bed, dressed and went to find the others.

I arrived late at the meeting, but luckily I made it. It was clear the other students had been waiting for me and were impatient. A select group of students was gathered in the headmaster's office. They'd been chosen to represent the school on a field trip to the Kigali Genocide Memorial to learn about the history of the Genocide and it's origins of the conflict. Apparently, I wasn't on the original list of students who were chosen for the trip, but when the headmaster arrived for the final debriefing he was frustrated I was not in attendance. He wanted me to be a part of the group.

"We can't go without Dydine," he said. "She is the most influential student here. Where is she?" That's when the headmaster sent the boy to my dorm to make sure I was a part of the group. And so I was added to the list of thirty other influential students who were chosen to learn about "Peace building Education." This was a new government-instituted program for high school students who wanted to learn about peace-building, at least so I thought. The idea was that we would then go back and train the other students from our school, teaching them what we learned.

The school had not only selected Genocide survivors, but students of all tribes and origins. We were all chosen to learn about the history of the Rwandan Genocide, the history that Rwandan educators were unsure how to teach to a new generation.

"You're very lucky to have been selected for this," the headmaster intoned. "This trip could change your lives."

I was honored to have been singled out yet again by the headmaster, but I was skeptical of the program's mission. Nothing the government had designed for us before had ever helped heal the wounds of genocide. I wasn't sure why this would be any different. Kigali was my home now, and the Genocide Memorial Center was only a twenty-minute drive away from us, but I'd never been before. I had never wanted to go! Why would I choose to relive those painful memories? I was certain there was nothing the center could teach me I didn't already know. I was eighteen years old by then, and already feeling weary of the world. I'd seen and experienced a lot of life and so much of it had been painful.

When we arrived at the memorial center in Gisozi, Kigali, everyone was silent. We were told to be quiet and to pay attention to our guide, who walked us through the memorial and explained the history of the Genocide. So many people were going in and out of the memorial, people from all over the world speaking different languages that sounded both harsh and musical to my ears. We reached a building and paused outside it. Our guide wanted us to enter one by one, to have time alone to process what we were about to see. This frightened me. I didn't know what I was about to confront, and I definitely didn't want to be alone with my emotions to contemplate it.

I was the last one to go in. At first, it was awkward for everyone. We wandered into an open room with walls lined with photos of the devastation. Then we all sat and the guide began to tell us where the Hutu/Tutsi conflict came from. Suddenly, everyone seemed awake. We never knew the history behind the hatred. It was simply something we'd grown up accepting: Hutus hate Tutsis, and the Tutsis hate them back.

I was shocked to hear that in Rwanda's early history, there had been no tribes. It's impossible to overstate the effect this had on me. It was like everything we'd been taught about who we are had been a lie. We started asking a lot of questions. Most of my fellow students were excited, but I was overwhelmed. I tried to quietly slip away from the group but got lost and found myself in the children's room. It was a circular room, filled with photos of children. The children were beautiful, and captions beneath the photos told their names, what they loved and what their dreams were. And then their last words before they were killed. Most of them begged for their lives. "Please forgive me," was a phrase I saw over and over along the walls. But there had been no mercy for them.

Whenever I turned my head to look away, I was confronted with a new face, a new story. The children smiled in all the pictures. Their faces were so full of joy and light. I felt such despair that I sat down and buried my head in my legs, and all my memories came rushing back. I saw myself at three and half years old, lined up in the neighbor's yard. I felt the cold glass of the jar of milk I'd clutched in my hands. I thought about how easily, how quickly, I could have become one of these children. For the first time, I cried about everything.

I cried and talked to myself simultaneously. It was an awakening. *Dydine, you survived. Look at these children. They never had the chance to grow up and work hard and realize their own dreams. They didn't have a chance, but you do. You've been feeling so sorry for yourself, blaming everyone else for what's happened in your life, but you have a chance. You can make the choice to change everything.*

I sat there for a while, running these words over and over through my mind, until one of my friends came to find me and tell me the second session had already started. When I stood up, I was a different person. My experience in the children's room transformed me. I knew, without a doubt, this would be the most memorable day of my life. It was the day I realized how fortunate I was. My life no longer seemed a curse, but an opportunity. I vowed from this day forward, I wouldn't blame others for my fate or my failure to shape my destiny. I would live life joyfully.

I returned to the training room and joined the other students. I listened carefully to the guide, trying to absorb all that I was learning. That day, I shared my own story with my fellow classmates. It was as though a weight was taken from my shoulders. That old familiar bitterness inside me was gone. I felt tapped, and emptied, emotionally exhausted, but finally free. I felt cleansed. Instead of focusing on my past, I turned my eyes toward my future.

The training completely changed my outlook. I realized the myth behind the Hutus and Tutsis races. We were not separate peoples, as I'd always assumed, but simply different social classes of the same people, an old, irrelevant designation created long ago, before the colonies. I asked many questions and was amazed to think that the hatred and conflict in my country could have stemmed from such a very small thing.

When I returned to school, I couldn't wait to share what I'd learned with my fellow students who hadn't had the chance to visit the memorial. I felt more responsible and motivated to spread the news of peace building, reconciliation and unity. Some of my close friends didn't quite understand me. They couldn't understand how I was changed in that short period. I had to do what I had to do. I was feeling it; this message was flowing in all the vessels of my blood. I knew that I controlled my destiny now. For the first time in a long time, I was excited for the future.

A year later, in 2011, I graduated from high school and started a new journey in life. It was such an exciting time, and I felt tremendous pride as I accepted my diploma. Then, once things died down and life returned to normal, I found myself with nothing to do. In all my eagerness to embrace the future, somehow I hadn't quite prepared a plan for what to do next. I loved being at home again, but without any real responsibilities, I soon became bored and listless. I did my chores and helped my mom around the house. Occasionally, I saw my friends, but it was painful for me to be around them as they spoke excitedly of their plans. Most of them were going to college, and I had nowhere to go.

I began avoiding them and spent most of my free time with my siblings. Fils was also about to finish high school, and he announced he wanted to continue on to University. I knew he was smart enough to do it. With his good grades, he was certain to win a scholarship. I had also hoped to go to university, but my family had no money to send me, and I hadn't received any scholarships. Besides, the area of study I was most interested in, art and film, was not offered in Rwanda. I would have to find another vehicle for my passions.

Luckily, fate smiled upon me. A small film company in Kigali had heard about me through a friend from high school. They knew about my song writing and singing, and they invited me to compose a song for one of their short films. I couldn't believe my luck; someone was actually asking me to write a song! I said yes without a second thought. When I asked when I should start, they told me to come in the next day. I arrived early the next morning and sat in the lobby, waiting for someone to tell me what to do.

The lobby had a round red and grey couch, surrounded by small tables covered with entertainment magazines. The walls were lined with film posters and photographs of famous movie stars. Eventually, the manager of the film company, a slim dark-skinned man named John, greeted me and invited me into his office. He asked me about my skills, and I told him about my writing, how I could sing and compose songs and also do some acting.

"I can do just about anything," I told him. "I just want something to do!"

John smiled. "Our company is small, and we are all Rwandan. We want to work with young people like you, who are passionate and willing to do everything they can to realize your dreams. We offer workshops. If you want, I can show you around and introduce you to everyone."

We walked around the office, meeting everyone in the film company. They were all young men, and I realized I hadn't even seen another woman since I'd stepped in the door.

"Do any women work here?" I asked the manager.

"There is only one, and she's not here," he replied. "You'll meet her next time."

Each person I met greeted me warmly and asked me about myself. One man asked me what languages I spoke, and when I responded that I spoke French, Kinyarwanda, and Swahili, the manager made a soft clucking noise and shook his head sadly.

"So disappointing," he said. "I was hoping we could have you work with us, but in our company, you must speak

English. We work closely with Americans and other international filmmakers, and there's no way you can communicate with them if you don't speak any English."

My heart sank. I could barely speak any English, and I realized I wouldn't be working at the film company anytime soon. I didn't know English, but I could still compose a song for their film.

I spent a week working with the producer, working on the song and observing how the film industry worked. I walked several miles to get there each day, and as I walked I thought up a never-ending list of questions. I'm sure my curiosity annoyed some people, but I didn't care. I was learning so much, and I was so inspired. For the first time, I really considered the art of film and what a beautiful, fun way it was to share stories. I learned how to write professional scripts with software like Celtx.

Writing had always been my passion, but I never dreamed it could also become a career. I had always loved sharing stories through writing. After composing a two-page song for the film, I realized I could write a twenty-page story, or even a hundred-page story. It gave me the confidence to imagine that I could one day write a book.

I knew what my book would be about: my country, its history and the capacity for goodness that resides within us all. I began sharing some of the writing I'd done in high school with my new friends on the film set. They were supportive and enthusiastic about my work. My mother wasn't happy with the arrangement; she worried I was wasting my time. Our home life was still so fragile. She had started receiving calls to get out of the house, and I'm sure she was hoping I might find a permanent job so I could begin helping with the rent. One day we were all watching TV when Mom received a call from the owner of the house. *Two weeks,* he said, *then you're out*! Mom slammed the phone on the receiver and burst into tears.

We were startled and scared to see our mother fall apart. We surrounded her, trying to comfort her, when the phone rang again. We froze, terrified the owner might have changed his mind and decided he wanted us out right away. Mom wiped her face and picked up the phone. We tried to read her body language for any hint of what was being said. The suspense was almost unbearable. She spoke for several minutes, or rather she listened, not saying much. *Uh huh*, she said. *Yes, I understand.* After she hung up, she ran into her room, all four of us chasing behind her. She sat on her bed with her face turned towards the window.

"Mom," I said, sitting carefully beside her. I touched her shoulder. "What is it?"

She started laughing, first quietly and then so loud and hard her shoulders shook.

I thought she'd really lost it then, and I looked to Fils in confusion silently asking him "*now what do we do*"? He shook his head at me. We'd never seen Mom react this way before.

"Kids," she said, catching her breath. "Maybe today is our day after all. God never turns his back on his children. That was an old friend. She's in the film industry. They're casting a new movie, and she thought I'd be a good fit for one of the roles."

"You? Acting?" I blurted. I couldn't imagine Mom being an actor.

Mom grabbed my face in both her hands and kissed me. "Dydine, I'm so happy, I feel like I could fly."

"Mom, this isn't going to work," Fils said. "I mean acting? Like Rambo, Jean Claude van Dame, Commando or Billy ? You're too old for that mom."

"Not every movie has explosions, Fils." Mom laughed. "Besides I used to perform onstage with the RPF Inkotanyi. I was pretty good then."

Bettina spoke up then, her voice high and sweet. "Mom, you're going to make it. I'm going to have a star for a mother."

Mom pulled Bettina into her arms and covered her face with kisses. "I love you, Bettina, you are the only positive person in this house. I'll take you to the premiere!"

Mom jumped up and began rifling through her closet. "I need to get dressed. They need me to come audition right away. Does anyone have some coins? I need bus money."

We checked our pockets and put all our coins together. It was just enough for Mom to buy her ticket. We wished her luck and once she was out the door, we burst out laughing. It was too crazy to think of our mother as an actress. We never thought they'd cast her. We returned to watching TV and waited for Mom to come back. The hour grew later and later and then finally, just as I was truly becoming concerned, Mom walked in the front door, carrying several grocery bags. She called me over to take one of the bags, and it was stuffed with delicious foods. Something good had happened. She'd gotten the part! We danced around the kitchen, preparing a late dinner. That evening, we celebrated her new career and went to sleep tired and content.

That first role and the money she brought in re-ignited a spark in my mother. Light started coming into our house and we even began to talk about our dreams again. Suddenly, nothing seemed impossible, because the impossible had happened! Mom asked us what we wanted to be when we grew up, and we realized we were allowed, and even encouraged to think about our dreams. The whole thing was so amazing and surprising. Only Fils seemed immune to Mom's new energy. He didn't want to share his dreams with us. He listened to us calmly, a bemused expression playing across his face as though he were surrounded by crazy people.

Encouraged by our change of fortune, I wrote my first short script and did all I could to bring the film to fruition. I wanted the film to capture the lives of my colleagues at school. A large part of the film was about HIV, how it was contracted and how it could be prevented and treated. HIV was a major issue in our country, and the film was designed to educate and help people. Every step of producing the film was a challenge. I had no budget, no equipment, no crew, but I wouldn't give up. I asked all my friends to come and act in the film. Finally, once everything was ready to film, I learned there were special permits I needed to secure from the government.

The Rwandan Ministry of Sport and Culture had to review and approve everything before they'd grant permission to film. The first time I applied for the permits, I was told that I had to be part of a company or an organization in order to obtain a filming permit. It was a crushing blow. I couldn't accept that after all my hard work organizing the film, it had all been a waste. I wracked my brain for a way to continue the project. I wasn't affiliated with any company and had few connections in my community. The situation seemed hopeless. Then, an idea came to me.

The next day I went to see a good friend of mine who owned a computer, and I asked him to help me design a logo. I knew no company would hire me in time to take my film forward, especially when I didn't speak English, but no one could stop me from starting my own company. I had volunteered in small companies before, and I knew a little bit about how they worked. I wasn't sure which next steps I should take, but I was determined to bring my dreams to reality. I wanted to become someone. I wanted everyone to see me as a talented woman who could make a difference in the community. And so I started my own business, Umbrella Cinema Promoters, with the mission of encouraging young women at home and abroad to share their own stories through film and storytelling.

At first it didn't quite seem real, but the more I thought about running my own company and what I wanted that company to be, I knew I wanted it to advocate for women. A woman had raised me, and I saw how talented and strong my mother had been and how hard she'd fought to keep us all together. I thought about how the first film company I'd written the song for hadn't had any women in their office, and how often women's stories were under-represented in my culture. The value I gave to women didn't seem to be the same value the rest of the world gave women.

I wanted to stand up for myself as a young girl, when I mistakenly believed I had no control over my future, and give other girls hope that they too had the power to change their lives. I wanted a logo that spoke to the value of a woman. We designed a logo of an orange umbrella with a woman sitting peacefully beneath it. When people ask me why I chose an umbrella, I answer that I want to be able to give them a detailed image representing the protection of women, while promoting and giving them a space to tell their stories.

I thought of my friends in high school who sold their bodies in exchange for pocket money, and I thought of the women who had been raped during the Genocide. Women seemed to suffer so much in times of conflict. I was constantly hearing their testimonies in the news, and the unfairness of their circumstances filled me with rage and frustration. I thought hard about how we as women could support and uplift one another. The power of my feelings motivated me to finish the logo, print out business cards and re-apply for the film permits. I knew what I wanted to do now. I decided that the next day I would tell my mother.

I walked to my mother's room and knocked twice. She was in a deep sleep, but finally opened the door for me, and asked why I was waking her so early in the morning. She must have seen the seriousness of my expression. She asked me to sit at the bottom of her bed and asked me if I was okay. I clutched my business card in my hand.

"I have something to tell you, Mom." I said.

"Go ahead, honey," she said, pushing the pillows up behind her.

I took a deep breath and told her I was starting a company. Mom smiled. "Is that why you woke me up?" she asked. "You are crazy. Go back to bed, Dydine! Don't bother me with nonsense so early in the morning." I stood my ground and explained I was serious. I showed her my business card and told her about my mission. She laughed at me. "You don't even have money for transportation to get around town. How are you going to start a company?" Her expression shifted to tenderness. "Dydine, I appreciate your idea, but now is not the time. You have no resources. Maybe you'll do it someday, but now is not the time." A deep sadness filled me as I left Mother's room, but in my mind I knew that nothing was going to stop me.

Dydine Umunyana

Later that same morning, I returned to my friend's house and borrowed his computer again. I asked him to help me add my new logo to letterhead, so I could re-apply to the ministry for the filming permits. I sat down and edited the same letter I'd submitted earlier that was rejected, but this time I composed it on my new company letterhead and listed my position as CEO on the bottom of the letter. Then I walked all the way to the Ministry of Sport and Culture to deliver it. Just one week later, I received their answer. They granted me all rights and permit to produce my film, and included a letter of recommendation I could share with anyone else I needed support from.

I am at the Kigali Genocide Memorial, in the children victims'
room

Chapter Twenty Three: The Leap

The same day I received the film permits and recommendation letter, I had an epiphany. The letter I held in my hands was the bit of encouragement I needed to propel me forward in my mission. It showed me that everything is possible. I thought about all the other young people in the country with so much talent and so much to give, but who perhaps were never lucky enough to receive such encouragement. For them, I vowed I would make the most of every opportunity that came my way.

I started reaching out to all my high school friends, asking them to join me in my cause. I was elated that they enthusiastically volunteered to take part. They assisted me with administrative tasks and together we held meetings to share ideas and brainstorm what to do next and to whom we wanted to reach out for support. I started attending conferences all over the country, learning more about Rwanda's history and meeting new people. Of course, I made certain I gave everyone my business card.

One of the conferences I attended was called Healing the Wounds of History. It was a two-day event held at a hotel in Kigali. One of my musician friends was the organizer, and he invited me because he thought it might somehow benefit Umbrella Cinema Promoters. I was surprised to learn that while the conference was about young people and how to invest in their futures so they could restore our country to greatness, there were very few young persons in the conference room. We made up only about 10% of the people in attendance.

We had no voice in the conversation even though all matters discussed concerned us. I couldn't wait for the Question and Answers session. When it came, my heart raced as I stood up to ask my question. My hands began to sweat and shake. I clenched my fists and took a deep breath. I asked the room why they were talking about young people and making decisions about us, when we were not represented. I told them it saddened me, because during and before the Genocide, conferences and movements were held by Hutu government leaders training young hutus people how to kill. And when the time came to punish the perpetrators, so many of those in prison were young people. They suffered the consequences, while the leaders who had trained them, made decisions for them and gave them their orders, often escaped punishment by fleeing to other countries.

"If this is the time to train young people about peace and love," I said, "we have to be here to participate in the discussion and add our voice to the decisions being made on our behalf. We are the energy and treasure of our country, if you will let us be."

I sat back and breathed a sigh of relief as applause broke out around me. One of the leaders of the conference thanked me for making such a strong point and assured me young people would be included as part of the decision making process. After the conference there was time to network, and people milled about the conference room making introductions and sharing contacts. I received a lot of business cards and people gave me excellent feedback on Umbrella's mission. Many asked me how they could help. Their response was so uplifting.

I felt what I was doing was important and making a difference in some small way. As I was leaving the conference, I crossed paths with a group of students from the University of Southern California. They were in Rwanda for the final year of their Masters program. We introduced ourselves and they asked me about Umbrella and what we did. I told them about our goal of giving voices to women in film, and that we had just started. I was startled when they told me they wanted to help me. At that point, I had everything ready to begin filming, but I didn't have a crew. *Our whole team is a crew!* They replied. They asked if I could complete production in one week. If so, they would be my crew and help me produce my first short film.

I simply couldn't believe it. Their generous offer of assistance was the most beautiful thing that had happened in my life. I quickly accepted and we made arrangements to meet the following day. I grinned the whole way home. I couldn't wait to tell my mother the good news. When I did, she immediately offered to help. Since she had been offered her first acting job, she'd made many new friends in the Rwandan film scene. She set about contacting all her friends and asking for production assistance. She enlisted her friends to come act in my film, and I confirmed the assistance of my own friends as well. It was a true community effort.

To have my mother's involvement and support meant so much to me. Since our earlier conversation in her bedroom, in which she'd laughed at my idea of starting my own company, she'd done an abrupt about face. In hindsight, I think she hadn't wanted me to get my hopes up. She was trying to manage my expectations so I wouldn't be disappointed if it didn't work out. When I actually began making inroads, and it seemed as though perhaps I could pull it off after all, she became my biggest cheerleader. Neither of us could quite believe our dreams were coming true. We'd become so accustomed to disappointment, it was hard to trust that good things were finally coming our way.

As production began on my first film, *What Goes Around Comes Around*, I realized I had no idea what I was doing. I didn't know anything about direction, or producing, but I tried not to doubt myself. I knew that I would learn it by doing it. At night, when I lay in bed worrying and all the thoughts of doubt played through my mind, I tried to take a deep breath and remind myself I was strong. I could do this. It was daunting, but it was also incredibly exciting.

My friends from USC proved invaluable. Some of the students were in theater programs and were good at acting. Others were Independent filmmakers. With everyone's talents combined, we were somehow managing to pull it off. The director of photography told me he was so happy to help me at the beginning of my career, because he was my age, 21, when he began. We worked days and nights for two days. When we finally finished, we sat down and celebrated. This was the first project of Umbrella Cinema Promoters. It will always hold a special place in my heart.

When the project was completed, we began screening it locally as an educational piece. I wanted to make a positive change in our community, to use my talents and the talents of my friends to teach other young people how they could share their own stories. I came up with the idea of offering a free workshop called "Women's Potential in Cinema." I wanted to teach local young women basic film skills such as scriptwriting, storytelling, photography and production, essentially all the tools and knowledge they would need to launch careers as filmmakers. I envisioned having twenty attendees, all women between the ages of 18-30.

This became Umbrella's second project. To pull it off, we needed funds. I registered Umbrella as an NGO (Non-Government Organization) with the stated purpose "to locate and identify young women who are isolated and need to use cinema to share their experiences, talents and feelings on how they overcame gender biased discrimination." And so I began the grueling work of applying for grants. I walked everyday to the printers to print letters, proposals and applications. In the end, I applied to over forty institutions throughout the country. Most of them said no, or made half-hearted assurances that they would support us next time. I hated those words: next time. Didn't they know that without their support now, there might not be a next time?

Every day, I opened email messages and letters that began with the word, "Unfortunately..." It was so discouraging;

I began to doubt myself once again. Some mornings I'd wake up not wanting to get out of bed. I felt like I couldn't face any more rejection, but I pushed myself. *Dydine, you have to do this. You can do this.* My friends also felt the effects of the rejections and began dropping out. They told me it wasn't personal, but each time someone quit, it felt like they weren't giving up on Umbrella, but giving up on me. I hated to even think about it, but I began to consider what I would do next if Umbrella were to fail.

I was walking around my neighborhood when my cell rang. It was a private caller, and I answered tentatively. A melodious female voice with an American English accent said, "Is this Dydine Umunyana?"

"Yes, it's me," I replied.

The voice exhaled with relief. "We've been trying to reach you by email for a while now, so we decided to try you by phone. I wasn't certain we'd ever reach you! This is regarding your letter for sponsorship for your organization's upcoming workshop. Are you available to come to the American Embassy tomorrow at 2pm? I would have been available at midnight if she'd asked me. I tried to contain the excitement in my voice.

"Yes, I'm available then.

"OK, arrive at 1:45pm for security purposes. Someone will be waiting for you, Ms. Umunyana. We look forward to meeting you!" No one had addressed me as Ms. Umunyana before. This sounded serious. I immediately turned home to tell my mother the news, although I wasn't sure if it was good or not.

The next day, Mother helped me choose a formal dress that would be appropriate for "Ms. Umunyana" to attend a business meeting. I took a bus to the Kigali American Embassy and arrived a full hour early. I sat outside the building, fidgeting, counting down the minutes until my appointment. When the time came, a security guard greeted me and ushered me through security. Inside, an American woman waited for me. She seemed surprised when she saw me.

"Are you Ms. Umunyana?" she asked, as though there must have been some kind of mistake.

"Yes," I replied, She eyed me up and down, but not in an unfriendly way. "Do you mind if I ask how old you are?"

I responded that I was twenty-one.

"Wow!" she said, her face breaking into a smile.

"From the work you're doing, I was expecting a much older woman. This is going to be fun."

Her friendliness put me at ease, but we rode the elevator together in silence. I caught her looking at me again from the corner of her eye, a smile playing about her lips.

When we exited the elevator and walked into the meeting room, I couldn't believe my eyes. The room was full of important people. There were representatives from USAID, the Public Relations Department of the Kigali American Embassy, and other prestigious groups. They all had files and notebooks and pens in front of them. I felt woefully underprepared. I hadn't even brought a pen.

Everyone in the meeting expressed surprise about my age. They peppered me with questions. *What inspired you to start an NGO? What are your goals? How do you choose who to support and who to work with? Where do you see yourself in five years?*

The first questions were the easiest to answer, but I stumbled at the last. I realized no one had ever asked me how I saw my future. For so long, it had seemed as though I had no future. I started by telling them what inspired me, and described our mission and goals. I could tell from the close attention they paid me, that they were following me, and as I continued, I gained confidence.

I couldn't wait to finish my pitch. It seemed like they truly understood what I was trying to accomplish. No one laughed. No one looked at me like I was trying to do the impossible. When the meeting ended, several people stood up to hug me. For a moment, I was confused. The woman who had greeted me in the lobby stepped forward.

"Congratulations," she said. "You've just been awarded a Grant for $5,000." Five thousand dollars! My mind reeled. In Rwanda's currency, this was over three million Rwanda francs, more than I needed to launch the workshop. I smiled nonstop. I thought I might start screaming my happiness right then and there. In shock, I somehow remembered to thank them before rushing from the room. I took their pen without even realizing it, and once I was in the parking lot, I laughed out loud for a few seconds and then called my mother.

"I'm so proud of you! I'm so proud of you!" she kept saying.

"I'm coming home now!" I told her. "I'll tell you all about it when we're together."

I greeted everyone who came down the aisle on the bus. I couldn't contain my happiness. I replayed the meeting over and over in my head. I would make the Kigali US Embassy proud,

I thought. I'd make them so happy they'd chosen me for their grant. With the money from the grant, I put together a team to run the workshop, and invited my new friend from San Diego, to serve as the main mentor for the project, along with two other Rwandan mentors. All twenty-four of our participants were women, most of them in their twenties, but a few in their forties as well. We had five days of extensive training, and then held a formal launch party for Umbrella Cinema Promoters at the Kigali Serena Hotel. Over one hundred people attended the event, and that same night I was approached by a British non-profit organization called Aegis Trust, which sought to prevent genocide against humanity.

I was startled to learn it was the same group that ran the Kigali Genocide Memorial, which I'd mistakenly assumed was sponsored by the Rwandan government. When I learned this, I told them about my experience visiting the Memorial for the first time, and how it completely transformed me. I told them it made me see young people in my country from an entirely new perspective, not the one based on whether they were Hutu or Tutsi, or where they came from, but one based instead on their talents and passions. That first visit to the Memorial had reshaped me into the woman I was today.

My conversation must have resonated with Aegis Trust, because shortly after the launch party I was appointed by the Aegis Trust, to be their youth peace ambassador. I could barely understand English, and I had no idea what a youth peace ambassador's role was. When I began asking questions, one of the directors stopped me short.

"It's up to you to figure out what to do, and how you should use our resources."

I still hadn't a clue, but I took a leap and accepted the offer. I understood all too well what a life without peace was like. It wasn't much to go on, but I thought our mutual goals formed the basis of a good partnership.

My affiliation with Aegis Trust launched me on a new path of research and discovery into the consequences of the Genocide, particularly upon Rwandan youth. I hadn't previously realized the extent of how many survivors families has been affected. During my research I met with another NGO called Kanyarwanda that was helping 530 local youths, offering them counseling, support and financial and educational assistance. All of these children had been born from rape. It dawned on me that not only were many young people suffering the consequences of the Genocide, but they were the consequences themselves. During the Genocide, rape was systemic and was used as a weapon by the perpetrators of the massacre. Because the subject was still so taboo (sex in general was not openly discussed in my country), it was impossible to say exactly how many women had been raped.

Most of these women had subsequently been killed, and many survivors still refused to speak of it. Thousands of children had been born from rape, and they needed a voice. Many of them grew up feeling unloved, or knowing nothing about their fathers. It was so hard for the victims of rape to love their children because their children were a constant reminder of what they had been through. Many victims later discovered they had contracted HIV. So many of the children from this NGO I met with were ashamed to be the children of militiamen, as though somehow their existence were their fault. They were often rejected by the community, reminded of their past every day as people reacted negatively to their very presence.

I learned that these children were often rejected both by the mother's family and by the father's, and that they were not considered survivors of the Genocide because, for the most part, they were born after December 31st, 1994. Thus, they were not eligible for government assistance with their studies from the National Assistance Fund for the Needy Survivors of Genocide (FARG). Hearing their stories made me realize that I was not the only one whose family was torn apart by the

Genocide. Many children had no family to speak of at all. I felt like it was my duty to share the truths I'd learned and help these children to love themselves and not be ashamed of their pasts. For me, the key had been in understanding that the important thing was the future, not the past. If we accepted and owned our pasts, we could begin to build better futures.

Through Aegis Trust, I began sharing my own story with small groups through a peace building education program. I started opening up about my past, although it took me a while before I became truly comfortable revisiting it in front of strangers. I took my duties seriously; I was determined to bring awareness and advocate for the Rwandan youth. I knew that sharing my story, however painful it might be for me, would help someone else who might be struggling with similar issues. I hoped I might give them the strength to hold on and to look toward a better future.

The role of Youth Ambassador suited me. I'd always wanted to be a fighter, a girl who didn't let anything take her down. My work helped me find solutions for myself, as well as for others. As I worked with Aegis, I continued to grow Umbrella Cinema Promoters. I committed myself to creating documentaries about my country's history, in particular about the Genocide.

It seemed I was always conducting interviews with survivors, Returnees, Perpetrators and Leaders hearing their testimonies. I thought about my father, and how he'd likely sat through similar stories as he presided over the Gacaca proceedings. It was easy for me now to understand how this work could bring one down. People endured hell during

Genocide against the Tutsis and somehow survived it, but they were never the same. Listening to perpetrators describe what they did and how they felt about it was chilling. There was no question, what happened to our country in 1994 still reverberates deeply today. We are all haunted, still trying to come to terms with what happened to us.

In April of 2014, I'd been working with Aegis for six months when I received another phone call that would change my life. It was Aegis Trust, asking me if I'd be available to come to the United States to work with them for three weeks in Los Angeles, spreading awareness about the Rwandan Genocide against the Tutsis. I said yes right away, not wanting to give them a chance to change their minds. I ran into the living room and told my mom. Without saying anything, she hugged me and we laughed and cried at the same time. I'd never imagined my work might open such doors of opportunity. I would walk through all of them with an open heart; I knew now with certainty, that anything was possible.

I am speaking at International Women's day Breakfast 2015

Afterword

My country's history is not unique. Genocide has occurred in Germany, in Cambodia, in Bosnia, Armenia, and it threatens to happen again today in Syria, Central African Republic, South Sudan, Burundi and in many other places around the world. Words cannot accurately describe what Rwandans endured during the days of the Genocide against the Tutsis in 1994, but I have tried to write honestly about my own experience and what the aftermath was like for those of us who survived. I came to realize that one's own life experiences are not theirs to keep but ours to teach.

I believe it's now our duty to share what happened to us and educate as many people as we can, in the hope that it will never happen again to anyone else. I know there is still much more work to do. Humankind continues to mistreat and be mistreated. For thousands of years, people have been immigrating, moving, fleeing, trying to find a place they can call home, to find a place that can fulfill their needs and make them feel safe. This is the way it has always been. It will always bring new difficulties, challenges, and hardships for some. It offers hope, and new opportunities for others. We must be wise and compassionate to meet these challenges.

In my life, I have encountered the very worst in human nature, but over and over again, when the days seemed darkest, someone extended a hand to me, or gave me some small gesture of kindness or encouragement that offered me hope for a better future. A friend of mine, Rita Kuhn, a holocaust survivor and author of *Broken Glasses, Broken Lives,* once told me, "When you take one life, you have taken the whole world. When you save one life, you have saved the whole world."

My hope for the future is to see more lasting peace everywhere-for me, my country and throughout the whole world. For many people, the word "peace" is a bit soft. It does not have a hard or tangible meaning. To me it is life, hope and joy. It is a wonderful, wonderful gift.

The atmosphere in Rwanda is hopeful but cautious. Since the time of Gacaca, between 2001 and 2012, some two million alleged perpetrators were tried. Gacaca may have brought justice for many victims, but it also re-opened wounds. We are healing, but each day we rise again to grapple with the past. Some perpetrators who have been forgiven and who have returned to their homes have continued to commit crimes against Tutsis. The government works hard to keep the people calm and encourage reconciliation and a culture of peace and love. We fight to reject fear and prejudice and to look toward the future.

I was able to travel to the United States in 2014, where I reunited with many of my friends including those at the University of Southern California. I began speaking publicly about my story at universities throughout the US, including the University of San Diego, Weber State University and the University of Texas at Austin. I've also appeared at the World Link annual event, at the Museum of Tolerance Los Angeles, at the Rotary Club in Santa Monica, and was the keynote speaker at the International Women's Breakfast.

In my talks, I share my mission, to inspire more openness and to build a lasting peace through a more inclusive society. My work with Umbrella continues.

After I conclude my school program in Film Production and Communication studies, we plan to conduct more workshops, and we have some larger projects in mind for the future. I continue to be an ambassador for Aegis Trust, and I am so grateful for this organization's impact on my life. Through their education model, which is based on a storytelling approach that shows examples of people like rescuers who have shown great courage and humility, I learned that leadership starts first with me. My life is an opportunity, a gift that can bring hope and good to those around me.

The Ministry of Education has adopted the peace education program from Aegis Trust and is now trying to teach it in schools. In the past, nothing about the Genocide was taught, because teachers didn't know how to handle it. The children of perpetrators and the children of survivors were together in the same class—how were teachers to address such sensitive material? Finally, teachers are receiving the training and support they need to tackle this difficult subject matter. I believe the more open we are about our experiences, the greater opportunity we have to truly heal.

My mother, Devota Benegusenga, is now a well-known film star in Rwanda. In the beginning of 2014, she was awarded with the first ever Best Female Actress Award at the Thousand Hills Academy Awards, a kind of Oscar Award across Rwanda. She has appeared in numerous local films, and recently wrapped up filming of a Kenyan TV series. In addition to acting, my mother started her own clothing design company under the name Umbrella Fashion Design, a move that helped keep my cause alive in my absence. She uses African breech cloth to make clothing for both men and women.

I consider my mother my best friend. Although we're far apart, we speak almost everyday. Our relationship has grown so that we are almost like sisters. We have apologized to each other for the mistakes we made in our most vulnerable moments. We are now closer than ever.

Aristide Kanamugire (or my brother, Fils) is a senior student at Adventist University of Central Africa (AUCA) in Kigali, Rwanda, where he is pursuing a degree in IT and Communication. He is quickly becoming one of the most talented web designers in Rwanda, and was recently awarded third place out of hundreds by MTN Rwanda for creating an app for mobile phones. Fils has also designed the web site of Kigali's local soccer team. His dream is to become a software engineer, and to help train other young people in programming.

As we were for so long as children, Fils is like my partner in crime. We are different people with different perspectives, but our skills are complementary. I like to lead and create ideas, and he is the practical one who implements them. We worked together on many projects related to Umbrella, and he was my assistant coordinator for our first workshop. Together, we make a great team.

Boris is a high school graduate who pursued Physics, Chemistry, Biology and Entrepreneurship as his principal subjects. While in high school, Boris was well known for his English language skills, and he won numerous awards and competitions for his competency for writing in English. He has also participated in peace building and conflict resolution campaigns, where he has acted as a counselor. A standout athlete, Boris is particularly passionate about basketball and continues to balance his studies with sports.

My sister Bettina is a senior high school student in Rwanda. She is currently pursuing History, Economics, Literature and Entrepreneurship. She was president of the Unity and Reconciliation Club in her former school and has participated in many debate competitions. She is also passionate about peace building and conflict resolution. Like me, she loves to sing and perform, and she composes her own music.

My father Laurent Kanamugire never recovered from PTSD, and we have had not been in contact with him since my mother moved me away with my brothers and sister to Kigali. I hope that someday he will find an answer to his suffering, and will find a way to heal.

I have shared my story, the story of my family and the story of my country with you dear reader, because I came to realize that one's life experiences are not theirs to keep but our to share and I want you to know that shadows are everywhere in life. But life is a choice, we should never resort to name-calling when we refer to others that we perceive as different from ourselves. Whatever color, religion, ethnicity or tribe you are or what part of the world you are from there is only one race, the human race. All that matters is what is inside you. Hate is not the answer.

There may be a shadow in your life, I do not know what your personal tragedy might be but I want to tell you that whatever happened has happened. What matters is what you do now and what you do next. Our individual light can become so bright that in our presence darkness disappears.

I have learned that we cannot do for others what we cannot do for ourselves. By nourishing the light within ourselves, we find strength we never knew was there.

The End

Mom with all her four children

Acknowledgments

*I am so grateful to the alMighty for giving me the strength to settle down and revisit all my cherished memories and share them on these piece of papers. Without the support, love and encouragement from all the people who have been in my life, I have no doubt that I wouldn't have been able to share with you my story. It is my great pleasure and honor to take this moment to thank you all from deep inside my heart.

*Writing this book required me to leave a part of my very soul within the paragraphs. It also became a way of healing unknowingly. I have come to a realization that it is not enough just to want to write a book; to put your words to paper. It is not enough just to be determined and driven to write a book; especially when you are a new English speaker, and you are writing it in English. It makes it much harder. But with my family, friends, and my editors' dedication of hours, soul, and talent, I was able to find the direction that was so needed to keep things on track. All their advice, criticism, ideas, and English correction helped me complete this book.

*To Mom, and my siblings; all my thanks go out to you. Mom, you are such an amazing parent moreover friend to me. All the love, courage and wisdom that you showed me, made me the person I am. Without your existence I wouldn't have all my wonderful siblings that I am very proud of. Thank you for filling in all my blank memories so our story can be well told and written. Thank you brother Boris for helping me in making corrections in this book, and not forgetting the map that you have drawn, which I have included at the beginning, and the end of these pages.

*Carol Seligson Fabi and Phil Israels Family; It is my great honor to express my gratitude to you, my wonderful friends that turned into family. You brought me in and embraced me with endless love for the last two years. I want to let you know that you gave me love, two beautiful sisters Giulia Fabi and Amy Israels, a wonderful brother, Sean Fabi, and friends. Words can never express how much you all mean to me. I am and always will be so thankful that our lives brought us together. You all have a special place in my heart.

*Michele Harell, Brent Swanson, James Smith, and the Smith family, Glen Ford, Nelson Paris, Jean Paul Samputu, and Michele Zousmer. Thank you for believing in me when I was a young girl trying to figure out what I wanted to become. You all shaped my destiny, helping me begin my career. You all have been wonderful friends and parent figures to me. Having you in my life has been a blessing. I just want to let you know that you are truly rare and wonderful people.

*To these who have been the best and most dedicated friends, I could ever have wished for, I feel so blessed to have you in my life. There are too many individuals, too numerous to mention in these pages. Your assistance, day in, and day out, made this book possible. To you, I would like to say thank you for everything: Christian Keller, Daniele Angeloni, Dominic Hoffman, Elizabeth Edelstien, George Karpasitis, Grace Rutagengwa, Ilona Brown, Jean Heath, Fredy Heath,

Johnny C. Lam, Kim Israels, Liz Lopez, Lydia Sarno, Maria Sarno, Moris Munyanah, Mucyo Philbert, Murenzi Kamatari, Nikita Mengue, Sally Harvey, Samantha lakin, Sandy Tmkin, Sabra Isimbi, Nadia Uwera, Dieudonne Sindikubwabo, Elizabeth Harvey, Elionora Granate, Kanamugire Aristide (Fils) Bettina Giramata Raissa, Jean Paul Ngiruwera, Karen Froming, Bill Froming, Patrick Manyika, Lourena Zondo, Roger Remera, Jeff Salz, Lisa Jaffe, Clementine Wamariya, Katarina Anais, Debbie Martinez, Stephen Smith, Heather Maio, Jeff Argend's Family, Michael Narvid, Mary Akpovi, Sharon Batamuriza, Kayumba Claver's family and all my friends throughout high school just to name a few. Everyone who has been in my life that is not on this piece of paper, you know who you are, and I am forever thankful to you too.

*Thank you to everyone who works at Zinqué in Venice California, a coffee shop that turned into my office for the last two years while writing this book.

*Last but not the least, I would like to express my huge appreciation to you my friends. This book could not have been in print without having all these special people with me through out my journey of writing it. When I thought of giving up or when everything seemed impossible, these people encouraged me and kept working so hard to make it possible: Barbara Kraft, Elizabeth Evens, Ariana Argend, Charles Ishimwe, Arno Michaelis, Consolee Nishimwe, Marian Coney, Amy Israels, Kanyamibwa Basil Boris, Kyle Ridley, Lisa Fruchtman, Rick Moskovitz, and Michele Harell. Thank you for believing in this book. It has kept me going even when things seemed bleak.

Author's Biography

Still in her 20s, Dydine Umunyana is the author of the book "Embracing Survival". Ms Umunyana was appointed a youth peace Ambassador in 2013 for the Aegis Trust, an organization dedicated to the prevention of genocide and mass atrocities worldwide. Subsequently, in 2015, she became a Global Mentor for Peace at Serve to Unite, an organization that cultivates peace through creative service learning and global engagement. Ms Umunyana is committed to establishing a dialogue between people for understanding their shared histories and culture differences. Through her writing and public lectures, her goal is to pierce the wall of silence that still pervades much of our society.

Resources

Kanyarwanda Association of Genocide survivors website

Genocide Watch website

United Nations website

Aegis Trust/ Genocide Prevention

Dictionary Thesaurus

Photographs

Page 49: washingtonpost website

Page 60: documentingreality website

page 68: historianerdicus website

Page 86: sassywire blog

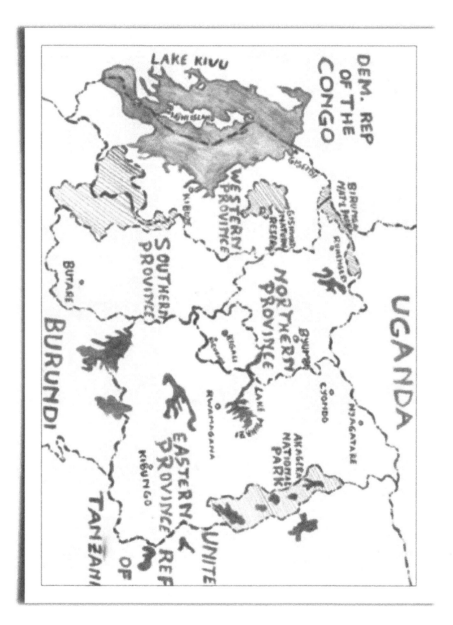